Information-Centric Networks

FOCUS SERIES IN NETWORKS AND TELECOMMUNICATIONS

Series Editor Marcelo Dias de Amorim

Information-Centric Networks

A New Paradigm for the Internet

Gabriel M. Brito
Pedro Braconnot Velloso
Igor M. Moraes

WILEY

First published 2013 in Great Britain and the United States by ISTE Ltd and John Wiley & Sons, Inc.

ISTE Ltd
27-37 St George's Road
London SW19 4EU
UK

www.iste.co.uk

John Wiley & Sons, Inc.
111 River Street
Hoboken, NJ 07030
USA

www.wiley.com

Library of Congress Control Number: 2013932267

British Library Cataloguing-in-Publication Data
A CIP record for this book is available from the British Library
ISSN: 2051-2481 (Print)
ISSN: 2051-249X (Online)
ISBN: 978-1-84821-449-1

MIX
Paper from
responsible sources
FSC
www.fsc.org FSC® C013604

Contents

Introduction

At the beginning of the Internet, users were academic in nature, mainly interested in mail exchange and file transfers. Furthermore, resource sharing was an important issue that imposed major challenges with regard to communication among end systems [JAC 09a, JAC 12, KUR 12]. Interconnected hosts should exchange data, such as files and database registers, and users had to access remote devices, such as printers and file servers. Thus, the improvement in communication efficiency among hosts was the main goal in this context.

Today, new technologies used by the network core and also by access networks has increased bandwidth availability, at the same time reducing users' access cost. The bandwidth increase has allowed developing a whole new set of applications, especially multimedia applications. The advent of these applications associated with the cost reduction has brought millions of new users to the Internet. Video-sharing Websites and file-sharing peer-to-peer (P2P) systems [MOR 08] are good examples of these new applications that are quite different from the first Internet applications. Both applications clearly indicate that the content distribution on the Internet has evolved from a textual information system towards a multimedia information system, in which data, services and applications are consumed as contents [PLA 05]. Currently, users are more interested in the content itself regardless of who sends it or its location. Documents, videos, audio, images, Web pages and metadata, for example, are "contents" [PLA 05]. This new scenario calls for the development of a network infrastructure that locally enables efficient and secure content distribution with high availability. The main problem faced today, however, is that applications are now content-oriented but the protocol stack remains the same, based on the content location.

There is no unique solution that addresses all the requirements of content distribution today. Basically, there are techniques that partially satisfy these requirements and overcome a few limitations of the current Internet architecture. P2P networks and content distribution networks (CDNs) are widely adopted solutions for distributing content, as indicated by the success of applications such as BitTorrent and CDN providers such as Akamai. Nevertheless, P2P systems and CDNs operate as overlays and, in general, do not take into account the underlying network topology to increase the efficiency of content distribution applications. In addition, the current Internet architecture experiences problems of content persistence, availability and security because the proposed solutions are very specific for a given problem and/or rely on proprietary mechanisms. Hypertext Transfer Protocol (HTTP) and Domain Name System (DNS) dynamic redirection, for example, are used by CDNs but do not guarantee content persistence. Queries to centralized structures are also needed in order to change content location, which increases the content delivery time [KOP 07]. Thus, it is clear that the current Internet architecture must change. This new architecture should take into account aspects to improve content location and delivery efficiency and also content availability. Fulfilling these requirements is the main goal of information-centric networks (ICNs).

ICNs introduce a new communication paradigm for the Internet. ICNs emphasize access to content regardless of its location. This is different from the traditional approach of the Internet, which is focused on the identification and location of end systems. The key idea of ICNs lies in using names to address content and to forward content on the network. Therefore, ICNs are based on novel concepts such as named content, name-based routing, security directly applied to contents and in-network caching [JAC 09a, KOP 07, VIS 09]. These concepts allow ICNs to deploy a more efficient architecture for content distribution, thus avoiding all the "patches" needed by the current Internet architecture such as IP Multicast, DNS and IPSec. ICNs natively provide new functionalities such as mechanisms to increase content availability, content security support and mobility support.

This book presents the main motivations for the ICN approach. First, the main problems related to content distribution in the current Internet are discussed in Chapter 1. The main techniques used to circumvent these limitations, such as multicast communication, P2P networks, publish/subscribe systems and content distribution networks (CDNs), are briefly described. Although these techniques provide a solution for content distribution, in general, they add much complexity to fix specific problems of the current Internet. The authors identify for each technique its main advantage and drawback, justifying the adoption of a new paradigm for the Internet.

Chapter 2 introduces the new ICN paradigm and presents fundamental aspects related to naming, routing and caching in ICN. The authors also discuss different approaches to these three aspects, showing the main characteristics and implications for the ICN. One important aspect is the use of content cache in the network core in order to decrease packet delay and load on servers.

Chapter 3 describes some of the main architectures currently proposed for ICNs. This chapter covers seminal proposals such as combined broadcast and content-based (CBCB) and state-of-the-art architectures such as content-centric networking (CCN), data-oriented network architecture (DONA), the publish/subscribe Internet routing paradigm (PSIRP) and content-centric inter-network architecture (CONET). Differences of naming, routing and caching approaches adopted by the different architectures are emphasized and so are the security aspects. Research projects under development to experimentally evaluate ICN architectures are also mentioned.

Chapter 4 discusses the challenges to distribute content in an efficient and scalable way and with high availability. The development of scalable naming and routing schemes, for example, is a great challenge. Routing decisions are made on the basis of content names and, thus, the way the names are defined impacts the routing efficiency. In-network caching also imposes new challenges to ICNs. Cache sizing, cache replacement policies, content placement and cooperative caching are a few open questions. This chapter also discusses security challenges, such as content authentication and privacy issues, requirements to adopt ICNs in wireless and mobile environments, and presents several applications that can benefit from adopting the ICN paradigm.

Practical issues are also fundamental to deploying ICN architectures on a large scale. In Chapter 5, the authors first present business models proposed for ICNs and then analyze hardware and software requirements to implement practical content routers. The main studies addressing practical issues are presented and discussed.

Finally, Chapter 6 points out new research topics and open questions related to the development of ICN architectures. These topics include inter-domain routing, interoperability between ICN architectures, standardization, peering agreements between service providers, content accounting, etc. These huge economic-financial challenges make the development of ICNs one of the most promising research areas and may potentially result in a radical change of the Internet communication paradigm.

1

Content Distribution on the Internet

In the beginning, Internet applications were based on textual information. Users were used to exchange email messages, transfer files via File Transfer Protocol (FTP) and access remote servers. Today, the Internet is a complex multimedia-information system based on content distribution. Documents, videos, audio, images, Web pages, for example, are "contents" [PLA 05]. Metadata used to find, understand and manage contents are also considered "contents". However, in order to enable users to request and receive contents efficiently, several basic requirements must be satisfied. First, content persistence must be assured. Persistence means that content identifiers[1] should be unique and valid during the lifetime of the associated content. Recently, with the advent of Web 2.0, the number of content publishers has hugely increased. Today, even users with low technical knowledge are able to publish content on the Internet easily. Thus, it is quite hard to assure content persistence in the current Internet. The second requirement is scalability. Content-search and forwarding mechanisms should be efficient regardless of the number of users and contents offered. Both must be able to operate at Internet scale. Finally, the secure access to contents is an important requirement to provide authentication and access control mechanisms to available contents. Currently, there is no solution that satisfies all these three requirements at the same time. Several techniques try to partially satisfy them

---

1 In this book, *identifiers* and *names* are synonyms.

and thus make the current Internet architecture more suitable to content distribution. In this chapter, a few of these techniques are briefly presented.

1.1. End-to-end concept and limitations

Three characteristics of the current Internet architecture are barriers to satisfy the requirements of content distribution: there are no guarantees of (i) quality of service, (ii) end-to-end security and (ii) no scalable forwarding mechanisms.

The Internet is a packet-switched network on a global scale, in which packets are forwarded based on the best-effort service model offered by the Internet Protocol (IP). There is neither resource reservation nor service differentiation during packet forwarding. Consequently, contents are distributed with no performance guarantees. Furthermore, the current architecture is focused on communication between hosts, which means that a source host includes in packet headers the IP address of the host that it wants to communicate with. Then, packets are forwarded hop-by-hop, based solely on the destination IP address. This paradigm is well suited for the first Internet application, because its main goal is to share remote resources offered by a specific host, such as a Web server, printer server and file server. Nevertheless, such a paradigm is not able to satisfy content distribution requirements, because it compels users to know not only where a content is located, but also the name of the content they want.

Currently, content distribution on the Internet is supported by "patches", that is a set of protocols and mechanisms that partially satisfy application requirements. The Hypertext Transfer Protocol (HTTP) redirect is an example used for searching non-persistent contents. With this mechanism, HTTP objects are requested by using resource locators, referred to as Uniform Resource Locators (URLs), which are in the headers of HTTP messages. Thus, HTTP redirect events are triggered by the server that hosted those objects originally. In this case, the server sends back to the client an HTTP redirect message containing the new URL in its header. This mechanism, however, must know where contents are placed and thus it is necessary to develop complementary mechanisms to assure persistent access to these contents, regardless of location, properties or other characteristics related to them. This example also illustrates how the client–server model works. In this case, one point-to-point communication channel is established between one client and one server. If several users simultaneously request a given content hosted by a server, multiple point-to-point channels are established and one copy of the same content is sent over each channel. Therefore, the more popular the content is, the less the efficiency of content distribution mainly in terms of bandwidth. Although not efficient, this model is widely adopted by the current content distribution applications. In summary, large-scale content distribution applications require the development of scalable forwarding mechanisms that must be quite different from the traditional client–server model.

Content distribution applications also try to provide content authentication and secure communication over the Internet. Currently, all of them employ mechanisms to provide a secure channel between the source and destination hosts instead of explicitly providing security to the content itself. Consequently, additional messages and process overheads are introduced [SME 09]. Internet Protocol Security (IPSec), for example, is a patch used to provide secure communication. Basically, IPSec allows users to establish reliable connections by introducing authentication headers (AHs), applying cryptography to data, using encapsulating security payloads (ESPs) and finally by employing key management mechanisms. In this connection-oriented approach, however, the content security depends on the trust of the host that stores this content and also on the connection established between hosts. Once again, scalability is the barrier to surpass. In this case, the same content are not available to be shared among different users, because the content is carried out within a secure channel between two hosts. The alternative is to establish multiple secure connections among content sources and different users, which are not scalable [SME 09]. Clearly, specific solutions for content distribution applications are currently mandatory.

1.2. Multicast communication

Multicast communication is one of the first proposals to increase the content distribution efficiency on the Internet. In practice, this technique is implemented by an IP multicast in the network layer [DEE 89]. Basically, with the IP multicast, one datagram sent by a host can reach multiple hosts that are interested in the same content. For that reason, these hosts are aggregated in a *group*, which is identified by only one IP address. Thus, if a host sends a datagram to the IP address of a given group, all the hosts that have joined this group receive a copy of this datagram. The role of the network layer, in this case, is to forward and replicate this datagram, when necessary, over the entire distribution tree that covers all the hosts interested in the group content. The advantage is to save bandwidth by not forwarding unnecessary copies of the same datagrams over one link.

IP multicast, proposed in the 1990s, is not currently adopted on a large scale on the Internet. For several authors, the main reason is the complexity to configure and manage the set of protocols needed by IP multicast. This complexity comes from the service model proposed by the IP multicast itself. In summary, a given host is able to join and leave a group at any time, it may be a member of more than one group simultaneously, and it does not need to be a member of a group to send datagrams to the group [COS 06].

1.3. Peer-to-peer systems

Peer-to-peer (P2P) systems aim at increasing content distribution efficiency by promoting content sharing among the users of the system. Basically, nodes interested in the same content, referred to as peers, create an overlay network at the application layer and altruistically share bandwidth, the process and storage capacity. Thus, they are able to exchange contents. The key idea is that each peer contributes to a given amount of its resources and uses the service offered by the system [PAS 12]. Consequently, the more peers there are in the system, the more is the capacity of the system to satisfy the user requirements (delivery time, content availability and among others). Thus, the scalability needed by content distribution applications is intrinsically provided by P2P systems. In addition, P2P systems do not require changes in the network core as IP multicast does.

Another key aspect is that users today are interested in receiving a given content – a file or a multimedia streaming – no matter who sends it. With BitTorrent, for instance, a new peer in the system randomly chooses its partners, that is the nodes allowed to exchange content chunks with it. These partners are selected at random from a subset of peers who are interested in the same content and no information about location or identification of peers is taken into account during the selection process. The huge success of both P2P file-sharing and P2P streaming systems – with millions of users – clearly indicates that the paradigm of the Internet application is changing. This is the basis for the development of Information-Centric Networks: users are more and more interested in the content itself and not in its sender.

Although scalable to distribute content, P2P systems suffer from security problems and the lack of incentives for peers to share their resources. P2P systems rely on the collaborative behavior of peers to work properly. Thus, the trust in data forwarded by other peers is a crucial point that must be taken into account by these systems. Another problem is the robustness of the system against peer churn, that is the capacity to deal with frequent arrivals and departures of peers. Peer churn may reduce content availability and distribution efficiency because there is no dedicated infrastructure to manage those events.

1.4. Content distribution networks

Content Distribution Networks (CDNs) are proposed to increase the efficiency and scalability of the client–server model employed by most of the content distribution applications today [PAS 12]. CDNs are composed of a set of distributed servers interconnected through the Internet that cooperatively work to distribute content [BUY 08]. Contents are replicated on different servers – preferably by different Internet Service Providers (ISPs) – and thus CDNs increase content availability and communication efficiency. Basically, CDNs redirect content requests to one of the replicas stored by a server closer to the requester. The main idea is to reduce the number of hops between clients and servers. Consequently, clients should experience low latency and high delivery rate because the congestion probability decreases.

Two building blocks comprise the core of a CDN: the distribution and replication service and the request redirection service [PAS 12]. Content producers use the distribution and replication service to find proper servers, to allocate storage capacity and, finally, to allocate contents to the selected servers. In addition, the request redirection service is the CDN interface with content consumers.

Basically, this service receives content requests and then forwards each request to the more suitable CDN server to satisfy it.

CDNs are typically composed of two types of servers: an origin server and a replica server. On the one hand, the origin server attributes the content identifier, stores and announces the content. Replica servers, on the other hand, forward the content to clients. In general, clients send requests to the origin server who redirects these messages to the replica server closer to the client and that stores the desired content. Figure 1.1 illustrates this process. In summary, redirection mechanisms severely impact on a CDNs performance.

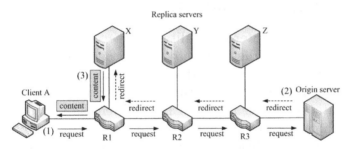

Figure 1.1. *A simple example of how CDNs work: (1) client A sends a content request to the origin server that (2) redirects this request to the replica server closest to A. Then, (3) X sends the content to A*

The simplest way to redirect requests in CDNs is to use the redirection mechanism originally offered by HTTP. In this case, all requests to HTTP objects are performed by Web browsers running on client hosts. When the origin server receives a request, it sends back to the requester an HTTP redirect message with the address of the best replica server. The origin server, in this case, is the bottleneck of the system and also a single point of failure because it processes all content requests. The Domain Name System (DNS) is also used by CDNs to redirect contents. Basically, the CDN DNS server receives messages requesting the address associated with the name of the origin server and then sends back to the client the address of the proper replica server. Both techniques – HTTP or DNS redirection – can select the "best" replica servers based on the number of hops or round-trip time (RTT) between clients and replica servers and/or based on the servers load. The main problem of these two techniques, however, is to guarantee content persistence. If the owner, domain or any other property of a given content changes, users may not be able to retrieve this content by using the same URL already known. In this case, for every change, users have to query centralized structures in order to obtain the new place of the content, which may increase the content delivery time [KOP 07].

The lack of interoperability between CDNs is another problem. Most of these networks are proprietary and specific for a given application and thus CDNs cannot be considered a general solution to satisfy the different content distribution applications on the Internet. In addition, server placement algorithms, capacity planning of servers and cache replacement policies have key roles on a CDNs performance [PAS 12]. For example, redirection mechanisms must select the best replica server in real time in order to have less impact on the delivery time, but it implies high computational costs. Also, the more the number of replica servers there are, the higher is the probability of finding a server close to the client. However, a CDN provider has to increase its budget to achieve that.

There are several examples of both academic, such as CoDeeN [WAN 04], and commercial CDN providers, such as Limelight[2] and Akamai[3], which are very popular. Akamai

---

2 http://www.limelight.com/
3 http://www.akamai.com/

has approximately 100,000 servers spread over the entire Internet, with points of presence in 72 countries and supports trillions of interactions per day [AKA 12].

1.5. Publish/subscribe systems

Publish/subscribe systems, or simply pub/sub, also indicates that the paradigm for current Internet applications is changing. Similar to P2P users, pub/sub users are interested in receiving the content regardless of its sender. In pub/sub systems, contents desired by users are referred to as *events* and the delivery of the content is called *notification*. The basic operation of a simple pub/sub system is the following. First, publishers create events and make them available to subscribers. Second, subscribers are able to announce their interest in events or event patterns defined by publishers. Thus, a subscriber is notified whenever an event that matches their interests is generated by any publisher.

Publishers and subscribers are decoupled in both time and space [EUG 03]. A subscriber, for example, may announce that it is interested in an event not yet published by any publisher. In addition, this interest should not be necessarily announced when the publisher is online. Decoupling, in this context, provides scalability to pub/sub systems because it allows publishers and subscribers to work independently [EUG 03]. Publishers add events to the system by calling the function `publish()`. Subscribers call the function `subscribe()` to register their interest in events. The pub/sub system, in this case, has a key role. The system itself have to store all interests announced and deliver contents to all interested subscribers, as shown in Figure 1.2. This operation mode allows pub/sub systems to distribute content between a huge number of users because publishers do not store states related to the interests of subscribers and subscribers receive content from any publisher, no matter if the sender is unknown [MAJ 09].

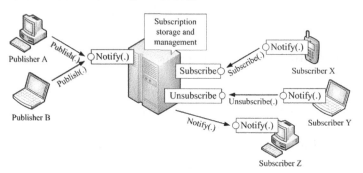

Figure 1.2. *Subscribe and event notification functions in a simple pub / sub system*

The first proposed pub/sub system is based on topics identified by keywords and is called a topic-based pub/sub system. Examples of this kind of system include enterprise application integration, stock-market monitoring engines, Really Simple Syndication (RSS) feeds, online gaming, among others [CHO 07]. With topic-based systems, users subscribe and publish events by using a topic, which is conceptually similar to the group defined by IP multicast, described in section 1.2. Each topic is a unique event service, identified by a unique name and provides interfaces to users that want to call publish and subscribe functions. Spidercast [CHO 07] and TERA [BAL 07] are examples of topic-based pub/sub systems.

Content-based systems are the next step in the evolutionary line of pub/sub systems. Basically, these systems allow users to subscribe to events based on properties of the events themselves and not based on previously defined and static characteristics, such as topic identification. With content-based systems, subscribers are able to specify filters to define their subscriptions by using restrictions based on attribute-value pairs (AVPs) and basic logical and comparative operators, such as $=$, $<$, $>$, $\leq$ and $\geq$. Restrictions can be logically combined by using Boolean operators, such as AND and OR, in order to define complex subscription patterns. These patterns are used in two basic functions of the system. First, patterns identify events of interest specified by a given subscriber. Second, notifications are forwarded through the system based on patterns, as detailed in section 3.1. Filters simplify the declaration of interests compared with topic-based systems. However, filters can introduce a communication overhead in the case of partially declared interests. Siena [CAR 01] and Kyra [CAO 04] are examples of content-based systems.

The different architectures employed by pub/sub systems can be classified into centralized or distributed, regardless of the way the subscribers specify their events of interest [EUG 03]. With the centralized architecture, on the one hand, event publishers send messages to a central entity that stores these messages and redirects them to subscribers on demand. With the distributed architecture, on the other hand, all system nodes must process and forward interests and notifications because there is no central entity. In general, distributed architectures rely on multicast communication and, thus, are prone to deliver content efficiently. In this case, topic-based systems benefit from this characteristic of distributed architectures. Content-based systems, however, face a huge challenge to efficiently provide multicast communication. Multicast performance is impacted by the computational cost of filtering needed during content forwarding, which varies with the amount of subscriptions in the system.

2

Information-Centric Networks

Information-centric networks (ICNs) introduce a radical change in Internet communications. ICNs emphasize information access regardless of location through a new data-based approach, allowing networks to actively deliver content. ICNs employ innovative concepts, such as named content, name-based routing, security mechanisms applied directly to content and in-network content caching [CAR 00, KOP 07, JAC 09a, LAG 10, DET 11]. All these concepts constitute many open subjects and challenges in ICNs, that are addressed in Chapter 4. This chapter introduces some basic ICN concepts and points out their advantages and disadvantages in comparison to traditional network architectures.

2.1. Content naming

As seen in Chapter 1, content retrieval over the Internet is intrinsically host-centric, which implies knowing the host IP address to send content requests to. *A priori* knowledge of an end system IP address is required to establish one or more communication paths between the user and content host and to allow content to be directly requested. This host-centric approach binds content to identification and location.

The ICN approach differs significantly from traditional host-centric network architectures. By treating content rather than its storage node as a first-class citizen in the network architecture [ZHA 10], ICNs allow content request and retrieval to occur in a name-based manner. This can be accomplished by using specific content naming schemes. An ideal naming scheme should provide names with the following set of features:

– *Uniqueness:* to assure unique content identification with the smallest possible false positives and negatives.

– *Persistence:* to guarantee the validity of the content name in synchronization with the content validity itself.

– *Scalability:* to allow different namespace scales, serving tiny and huge namespaces the same with no limitations regarding content nature, storage location or any other characteristic.

A number of naming schemes can be used to identify content and to directly request content distribution to the network infrastructure. Three basic content naming techniques can be used in ICNs: flat naming, hierarchical naming and attribute-based naming.

2.1.1. *Flat naming*

Flat names are randomly looking sets of bits used to identify objects. Flat naming schemes apply different mapping approaches to come up with flat content identifiers, a cryptographic hash function being the most common. Flat names can be considered persistent since they lack semantics, that is, there are no explicit rules to bind information into the content identifier format or meaning. There is no relationship between the content identifier and its location, provenance or any other characteristic besides the bond between content itself and its name. As an example, the SHA-1 hash function[1] maps words smaller than 2^{64} bits into 160 bit-long hash keys by applying many Boolean operators in different blocks of the original word [WAN 05]. This mapping depends only on the original word, returning a fix-sized key for different input lengths. Uniqueness is also granted given that the chosen hash function should have low mapping collision probability [PEY 98]. Since cryptographic hash functions return to fixed length keys from arbitrary words, a common aspect to most of the flat naming schemes is their fixed length identifiers.

Flat naming schemes allow self-certification of content and identifiers. By using pairs of cryptographic hash keys of the form P:L, where P is the cryptographic hash of the content publisher's public key [KOP 07] or content itself [DAN 10] and L is an arbitrary label chosen by the publisher, each node can verify the validity of keys used in content coding and in the binding between content and its name [GHO 11b]. In this way, users only have to trust the relationship between names and real identities of publishers for complete content certification. Since robust and scalable key distribution systems are a well-known topic, the usage of similar external trust mechanisms could be extended to ICNs [GHO 11b]. However, once cryptographic keys are used in flat names, they are not user-friendly, making external mechanisms for mapping user-friendly into flat names a must [KOP 07].

Flat names have one undesired characteristic: it is impossible to aggregate them into prefixes. This can lead to severe scalability issues to name-based routing protocols. Since flat names cannot be aggregated, forwarding and routing tables are required to have one entry per content name. This requirement introduces a new challenge to ICNs, which is the development of efficient flat routing in a global-scale network such as the Internet.

---

1 Available at http://www.xorbin.com/tools/sha1-hash-calculator/.

2.1.2. *Hierarchical naming*

Hierarchical naming structures have also been proposed for ICNs. By concatenating different string name components, unique identifiers can be formed and assigned to content. In opposition to the randomly looking names of flat naming systems, hierarchical names have intrinsic semantics since their structures and components reflect information related to the nature of the content itself: property, version, format and so on. Thus, structures similar to Uniform Resources Identifiers (URI) [MEA 02] can also be used to represent hierarchical names.

Access to dynamic content requires that users are able to construct, in a deterministic way, the names of the desired data without any prior knowledge of the name or content itself [GHO 11b]. Partial names and relative requests can be used to determine name sequences in a simple manner, exploiting the hierarchical relationships between name components. A user can request a content, for example `br.uff/video/intro.avi`, based on the composition shown in Figure 2.1 and receive a specific chunk of that content, called `br.uff/video/intro.avi/1/1`. In a second moment, this chunk could be used as a reference to select and request other chunks relative to the first segment, such as the second chunk, whose name is `br.uff/video/intro.avi/1/2`.

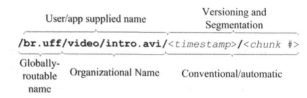

Figure 2.1. *Hierarchical name structured as a URI*

A direct consequence of using hierarchical names is the ability to directly aggregate them as search aggregates through longest prefix matching, similar to IP routing protocols. Thus, many of the mechanisms already proposed for dealing with IP addresses can be adapted to deal with hierarchical names, simplifying the process of gradual adoption of ICNs and reducing the burden on the routing protocols [JAC 09a]. Owing to the reflection of content properties within their name structures, hierarchical names do not have strong persistence. The semantics behind these names does not allow their persistent usage, since any change applied over content should be reflected in the name components, due to ownership transfers or other logical change.

2.1.3. *Attribute-based names*

Unlike other naming schemes, attribute-based naming does not provide a unique identification for each and every content. Attribute-value pairs (AVP) of the form [attribute = value] are assigned to content and make it possible to identify them. For example, instead of requesting a content by providing an explicit name, content is identified by certain attributes like [class = "alert", severity = 6 device = "web-server" type = "fault hardware]" and should be requested through applying constraints over them like [severity >2 ∧ class = "alert"][CAR 03]. The sets of constraints that can be used for identification of contents are called predicates [CAR 00]. There is a direct relationship between predicates, their sets of restrictions and the contents they represent, which is called coverage. A predicate is said to cover another predicate if and only if all content obtained by the latter is contained in the set obtained by the first predicate.

The predicate coverage property is what enables AVPs to be aggregated. Since predicates consist only of logical operators and AVPs, we can easily obtain aggregate predicates whose coverage includes several subsets of content. Another characteristic of attribute-based naming is the ability of searching content directly over the network infrastructure, without the need for external applications or mechanisms for this purpose. Once contents are not explicitly named, we can specify predicates that cover large sets of content, being the end user responsible for verifying what content satisfy its interest.

AVPs and sets of logical constraints as content names impose some challenges for ICNs. The first challenge is the difficulty in expressing the minimum constraint set required to precisely resolve content, which creates some barriers to uniqueness. Since predicates cannot exactly define the wanted content, users must treat the excess or lack of content available upon receiving time, impairing the performance of applications. The case of excess content delivery characterizes inefficient use of network resources, which propagates unwanted traffic on several branches of the network and delivers unwanted content to end user.

2.2. Content or name-based routing

Unlike host-centric networks, ICNs should be able to deliver content requested by name, without any information regarding its storage location. To this end, ICN nodes need information about existing content on the network to efficiently route content requests to valid copies of that content. This content or name-based routing should have the following characteristics:

– *Content oriented:* packets should be addressed to content names, without information about source or destination.

– *Robustness:* routing should be fault tolerant and quickly recover from discontinuities, avoiding sending data to faulty nodes.

– *Efficiency:* control information should have low impact on network traffic.

– *Scalability:* routing should be flexible so as to be deployed in a variety of scenarios, serving dense network topologies and large namespaces and tiny local networks as well.

Content routing, or name-based routing, has a number of particular characteristics regarding how the routing information is exploited by nodes and how such information is stored on the network. The mechanisms can be divided into two main groups: non-hierarchical routing and hierarchical routing.

2.2.1. *Non-hierarchical routing*

Non-hierarchical routing, or unstructured routing, lacks dedicated structures for storing routing information and do not organize routers in hierarchical structures. By establishing links between nodes on demand, according to instant content delivery needs, non-hierarchical routing allows all nodes to obtain valid content. Since there is no central or root node for routing information storage nor deterministic flows of control and data packets, routing information must be disseminated among nodes in a global fashion, allowing every node to calculate the best routes for content delivery, whatever criterion is used.

This kind of routing allows multiple paths to be used for the same content, once the knowledge of the entire network topology allows the calculation of loop-free routes and increases the availability of the network as a whole, because there is no single point of failure. Internet routing protocols are, in general, non-hierarchical. Thus, most of the problems encountered in these protocols has been identified and researched in the past, enabling them to be applied to non-hierarchical ICNs [JAC 09a, CAR 04].

2.2.2. *Hierarchical routing*

In hierarchical routing, or structured routing, network routers are connected in a hierarchical structure, ensuring deterministic flows of routing information and data. On the basis of the premise that routers are organized into several hierarchical levels, hierarchical routing protocols are able to reduce the amount of control information, exploiting the hierarchical relationships between these routers. ICNs have basically two hierarchical routing concepts: tree-based and distributed hash tables (DHT) architectures.

Hierarchical tree-based network topologies, as shown in Figure 2.2a), require knowledge of the location of the desired destination node. Concepts such as affiliation, parity, superiority and inferiority are intrinsic to hierarchical structures, which can be applied to named-based routing. Parent nodes are those that have connection with one or more child nodes, configuring the root of a sub-tree to which the child node belongs. Peer nodes are those nodes belonging to some hierarchical level, in relation to a common root node. Parent nodes concentrate all routing information from their child nodes, acting as gateways between the parent and the child sub-trees. Peer-node trees are directly reachable, and it is only necessary to resort to a parent or a higher hierarchical level router when the content request resolves to higher level sub-trees [KOP 07]. Parent nodes are required to aggregate the routing load for the entire sub-tree, decreasing the amount of information used by each child node in routing and, consequently, reducing their computational requirements, such as processing power and memory. Nodes do not have a complete map of the network topology, but require only to store routing information of their parent, peer and child nodes. Evidently, the parent node represents a single point of failure and can eventually cause the removal of entire branches of the content distribution tree.

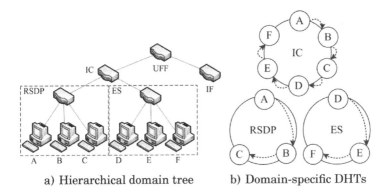

a) Hierarchical domain tree   b) Domain-specific DHTs

Figure 2.2. *Hierarchical tree and a DHT overlay*

DHTs are structures adopted for cryptographic hash keys distribution among participating nodes. Processing and caching costs involved in key mapping are shared among nodes, ensuring protection against single points of failure [GAN 04]. DHT-based hierarchical mechanisms, or hierarchical DHTs (H-DHT), allow us to arrange nodes in overlay networks, forwarding messages efficiently toward hash keys.

H-DHT structures ensure that all nodes in a specific domain are part of an exclusive DHT, so that higher hierarchical levels are a fusion of lower level nodes. For example, in the topology shown in Figure 2.2a), various hierarchical levels, or subdomains, make up the domain UFF. Nodes belonging to this network participate in each of the existing subdomains, such as RSDP and ES, sharing processing and resources among nodes of each different DHT, as in Figure 2.2b). Thus, node A communicates with nodes B and C in the RSDP domain DHT, whereas it communicates with nodes B, C, D, E and F in the IC domain DHT. H-DHTs provide fault isolation to the routing protocol due to load and functionality sharing among nodes. Once faults in nodes affect only a fraction of the keyspace, it can be rapidly redistributed among participating nodes [GAN 04], recovering the network.

2.3. Content caching

ICN architectures are challenging scenarios for in-network content caching techniques. On the basis of the Internet content access characteristics, in which a small number of popular content contributes with most of the traffic on the network [BRE 99], content replicated and cached in nodes closer to the users implies a large reduction in network traffic, improving service quality level [WAN 99]. Content routers can be extended to provide a distributed storage infrastructure, in the same way traditional CDNs do. As content is forwarded to different nodes, a router can store the most frequently accessed content in memory, operating as a cache network [JAC 09a].

The approach to content storage in ICNs differs from traditional solutions adopted by CDNs. In CDNs, besides evaluating content popularity by the amount of requests made on a real time and global scale, nodes cooperate in an orchestrated manner, conducted by a centralized management element to optimize resource utilization and replica distribution. In ICNs, the caching decision process is based solely on local information. Nodes take into account content requests and data delivered when determining which content to keep. In essence, any node of the network, including user systems, can act as a cache at any time, enabling existing networks to be extended into private and public content distribution networks, even on global scale.

Despite not dealing directly with the location of the content, the use of in-network caching eventually distributes copies of content to distant nodes, closer to the end users. This scenario leads to a complex problem that needs to be solved by routing protocols. As content route aggregation can get very complex under caching, the routing information structures' performance would quickly decrease and impact upon protocol efficiency.

3

Main ICN Architectures

This chapter presents some of the main ICN architecture proposals, focusing on how the basic content-oriented concepts are applied. Research projects developing and extending these concepts are briefly presented as well.

3.1. Content-based networking/combined broadcast and content-based

Content-based networking (CBN) architecture [CAR 00] is one of the first ICN proposals, heavily based on event-notification publish/subscribe systems. CBN is an architecture in which content is published without explicit receiver addresses, delivering it to all nodes that have declared an interest in receiving that content.

Each CBN node advertises a predicate that defines its interest in receiving messages called the receiver predicate, or *r*-predicate. Messages are identified by AVPs, as described in section 2.1.3, identified by attribute type, name and value. For example, a set of valid AVPs would be [string company = PET, int price = 30]. Predicates are usually represented by a set of restrictions, or Boolean filters, applied over these AVPs. The predicate [string company = PET ∧ int price <40], for example, covers the message just shown. Besides the r-predicate, nodes can issue a sender predicate, or s-predicate, defining content they intend to serve. An r-predicate, while setting interest for messages, can be interpreted as a content-based network address once it sets the necessary forwarding state in the network, allowing nodes to receive content. Thus, predicate issuing defines the concept of subscription. Constraints declared by an r-predicate, or a subscription, act as filters for flooded messages.

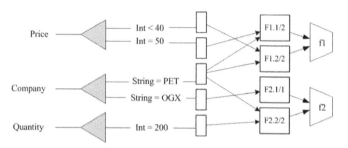

Figure 3.1. *Simplified forwarding mechanism [CAR 03]*

From a general perspective, a CBN routing mechanism can be interpreted as a mapping structure taking attributes, constraints and router interfaces as inputs. The routing mechanism is implemented as shown in Figure 3.1, in which all attributes found in received predicates are in the leftmost part or in the process input. Attributes are filtered under constraints defined by predicates and sent to proper interfaces according to some Boolean operations. Such operations implement conjunctions of constraints [CAR 03], establishing the necessary state for forwarding messages to the applicable output interfaces. Routing table information is provided by the combined broadcast and content-based (CBCB) routing protocol, characterized by a content-based layer deployed over a broadcast layer [CAR 04]. The broadcast layer treats all messages as broadcast messages, while the content-based layer dynamically prunes distribution paths, shaping the way messages are retransmitted. The broadcast layer ensures that all messages flow from the sending node to all receivers through loop-free and possibly shortest paths. This layer can be implemented using known mechanisms for loop-free topologies as spanning-trees, per-source trees and other diffusion mechanisms.

CBCB propagates routing information in two ways: by sending receiver advertisements (RAs) and sender requests (SRs). RAs are periodically issued by nodes and whenever they change, their predicates change as well. RAs carry new predicates, propagating this information to all potential content, provider nodes and creating the required routing state for proper message distribution towards receiving nodes. Whenever an RA is received in a given interface, the content router checks whether the advertised address is already covered by the receiving interface predicate. If this condition is true, the RA and the announced filter are discarded. If not, the router computes the set of interfaces belonging to the RA emitter-centered tree, sends the RA through such interfaces and establishes paths for messages to flow. The final step involves updating the routing table by logically adding the filters included in the RA to the predicate of the receiving interface.

Routers use SRs to obtain information about all the existing receivers, allowing them to update their routing tables. Upon receiving an SR, a node responds with an update reply (UR), containing all the predicates of its interfaces. Receiving an SR implies its immediate forwarding through all available interfaces within the source-based tree. In addition, nodes only respond with an SR to the originating node after they had received URs from all interfaces belonging to the source-based tree or after an expired timer.

The protocol also allows routers to cache and reuse URs, which reduces the amount of control traffic overhead.

The first implementation of the CBN content-oriented architecture was developed for performance evaluation of its concepts [CAR 03, CAR 04]. These studies showed that CBN/CBCB routing mechanism presents an acceptable performance even in scenarios where millions of possible constraints are applied. Experimental results indicate that the CBCB routing protocol is able to effectively deliver requested messages to receiver nodes. AVPs used to identify content, as described in section 2.1.3, have a drawback when it comes to uniquely naming content since predicates can cover one another. This implementation presented an acceptable false positive rate, which has generated a constant overhead traffic of approximately 10%, considering all sent messages. In addition, interesting properties were observed as control traffic volume being proportional to the rate of change of predicates and decreased node memory requirements due to the use of storage and reuse of URs, providing some scalability to the architecture.

3.2. Data-oriented network architecture

Data-Oriented Network Architecture (DONA) [KOP 07] is the first information-centric architecture based on clean-slate concepts for secure and persistent content naming, name-based routing and content distribution in a hierarchical network. DONA provides persistence and authenticity to content by using self-certifying flat names. The routing mechanism guides content requests to the best serving nodes, avoiding faulty or overloaded nodes.

Every DONA name is generated by a principal, or publisher, an entity associated with a public–private key pair, which is used to identify content. This association is critical to DONA naming. The names have the form of P:L, where P is the cryptographic hash of the principal's public key and L is an arbitrary label, chosen to ensure uniqueness of the name. Principals have the role of content administrators, where once only allowed nodes, those which have access to the key associated with P, can provide access to named objects of type P:L. In response to their content requests, users receive data, a public key P, a label L, metadata and a signature [GHO 11b], allowing them to immediately check the data authenticity. This is accomplished by verifying that the hash of the public key is indeed P and that it was used to sign that content. As flat names of the P:L form are composed by random-looking strings of characters, there are drawbacks related to the end users handling of names. DONA considers that users get names through various external mechanisms, such as search engines, private communication, recommendation services and other existent trust and recommendation systems.

The name resolution mechanism, that is, content requests routing, is implemented on nodes called register handlers (RH), which implement a very simple yet effective protocol. FIND(P:L) packets are sent to the local RH to locate the specific object P:L. The RH, in turn, forwards the request toward the node holding copies of the requested content. REGISTER(P:L), sent by nodes desiring to provide copies of that content, establish the necessary state for RHs to effectively forward FIND packets. Nodes duly authorized by the principal can also send REGISTER(P:*) packets to their local RH. Thus, regardless of the L label used, every content request under the principal's P key will be sent by local RH to the node that registered P:*. The RH maintains separate entries in the routing table for P:* and P:L, resolving possible different next hops for each entry. The existence of entries in the routing table is crucial for routing FIND packets to the closest copies of the content. The absence of an entry in the table makes the RH forward the FIND packet to a hierarchically higher RH node, eventually finding a valid entry in its routing table since higher RHs concentrate routing information from their children nodes (or subdomains).

DONA, in similarity to the CBN architecture described in section 3.1, does not entirely discard IP technology. The FIND packet is characterized by its insertion between the IP and transport layer headers, limited to content address resolution. Thus, conventional transport mechanisms are triggered to perform content delivery, only guiding those name-based mechanisms without major changes in protocols and the infrastructure that supports them.

Automatic server selection, a desired feature in any content distribution system, is natively supported in DONA. RHs forward FIND packets to the lowest cost neighbor, according to any chosen delay metric. Multi-homing and mobility are also intrinsic to DONA. FIND packets may be routed to more than one node by a multi-homed RH, resulting in the use of multiple paths for requesting content. The content registration protocol, based on REGISTER and UNREGISTER messages, is responsible for providing mobility to end systems, since nodes can unregister their content addresses prior to changing their position in the network topology, registering them again after properly connecting it to their new location. Once new registers have been published and established the required forwarding state, all FIND packets will be routed to this new location. Multicast content distribution is also naturally possible due to the use of P:L identifiers, the L label being the identification of a multicast group, providing means to create source-specific groups of the form (S,G), similar to a source-specific multicast (SSM) [BHA 03, HOL 06].

Some optional extensions were proposed to DONA, extending even further its impact on content distribution.

In-network caching in RHs extends their functionality by implementing a generic and always-on content caching infrastructure in the content distribution paths, providing better quality of service. Long-term content subscription and update notification can be achieved via Time-To-Live (TTL)-added FIND packets. While the FIND is valid, relevant updates will be sent to the interested node. Another feature is the ability to avoid faulty or overloaded servers, as previously cited. Nodes can include cache, network and processing load information into REGISTER packets, providing sufficient information for the routing mechanism of FIND packets.

3.3. Content-centric networking/named-data networking

Content-Centric Networking (CCN) [JAC 09a] adopts named content as a first-class citizen, addressing subjects such as high availability and security in a content-oriented fashion, regardless of location. CCN, in analogy to the previously presented proposals, preserves some of the concepts that made Transport Control Protocol (TCP/IP) simple, robust and scalable, extending them to provide a flexible network layer with fewer requirements to the data link layer.

One of the CCN's main features is the division of content into chunks, named objects with unique and hierarchical identifiers, which can be individually requested. CCN names are composed of a variable number of components, exactly as presented in section 2.1.2. Each component is formed by an arbitrary number of octets, transparent to the transport layer, and may even be encrypted. An advantage of using hierarchical names is the ability to aggregate names by referencing them through the longest possible prefix, the root of a name component tree. Hierarchically structured names also allow relative referencing to objects within the hierarchical structure, including defining the position relative to different levels of the name tree. For example, in the name tree shown in Figure 2.1, content can be requested by its absolute position, as in *br.uff/video/intro.avi/1/previous*, requesting the previous version, or as in *br.uff/video/intro.avi/1/1/next*, requesting the next chunk. Data are said to satisfy the stated interest if the name of the content in the interest packet is a prefix of the one in the data packet. This is the same as saying that the chunk's name in the data packet is in the name subtree specified by the interest packet.

CCN architecture is based on two basic primitives: an interest statement for a specific chunk and the transmission of this chunk in response to the interest. Users request content directly to the network by broadcasting their interest for a certain chunk, in the form of an interest packet (I-packet) on all broadcast available interfaces. Nodes send a data packet (D-packet) in response to the I-packet in case they have the requested chunk stored locally. Otherwise they forward the I-packet to their neighbors until it eventually reaches a node caching the data. Data are only sent in response to interests, consuming the equivalent pending interest on each node in the reverse path.

Packet forwarding in CCN is strongly derived from the IP, basically a mapping between the content name and the output interface associated with the packet distribution tree, with some special features. Each router uses three distinct structures in the packet forwarding process: the content store (CS), the pending interest table (PIT) and the forwarding information base (FIB), illustrated in Figure 3.2. FIB is a database used to store packet forwarding information, performing the mapping between content names and one or more output interfaces, allowing multiple source routing. CS is the cache structure in a CCN router, storing chunks for the longest possible time by applying cache update policies similar to Least Recently Used (LRU) or Least Frequently Used (LFU) [POD 03]. The PIT is a table in which are registered interests forwarded ahead, keeping record of the source interface so that data can be sent back in response. Upon receiving an I-packet, the CCN router first searches in its CS for an entry related to the requested content. If such entry exists, it sends back the proper D-packet. With no CS entry, the router checks if there is a pending interest in the PIT for this content. If so, the receiving interface of the I-packet is added to the list of interfaces for sending content in PIT and the I-packet is discarded. If there is no entry in the PIT, the router forwards the packet according to the rules of its FIB, creating a PIT record for the source interface. If there is no entry in the FIB for a certain content, its interest is discarded since there is no valid forwarding interface. Such diffuse routing aims to eventually find a node that can respond and send the data packet in the reverse path, signaled by the PIT entries in each hop. Only a valid PIT entry leads to the D-packet forwarding, with all the other scenarios leading to the packet disposal. Data sources are required to register their intention to provide content through a register primitive, creating the initial required forwarding state.

Strategy layer implements the packet forwarding decision-making mechanism used by CCN routers, dynamically determining how a router forwards interest packets. Unlike TCP/IP, the strategy layer of the receiver node is responsible for re-requesting undelivered or corrupted content. Flow control is also implemented by the strategy layer since sending multiple sequential chunks in parallel has the same functional behavior of the TCP window, which controls the amount of traffic that data sources can insert into the network.

CCN naming and forwarding schemes have roughly the same characteristics showed by traditional location-based network mechanisms, allowing any valid IP routing scheme to be used as a potential solution to CCN routing needs. CCN forwarding does not impose restrictions in using multiple sources or destinations for a given content since PIT entries prevent formation of loops in the network. Hierarchical names, with semantics similar to that of IP addresses, allow aggregation of content names and the usage of the longest prefix match.

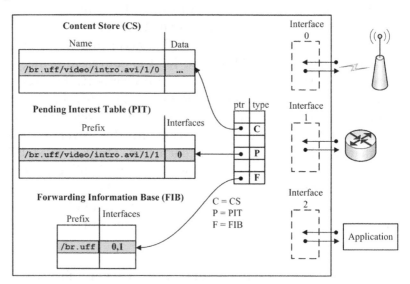

Figure 3.2. *CCN node and its forwarding structures, as presented in [JAC 09a]*

CCN security mechanisms are directly applied to content regardless of what mechanisms are adopted by the transport layer. Through signing content, using the name and the content data as inputs, the publisher authenticates the binding between name and content. This binding allows publishers to assign arbitrary names to their publications and makes them easily authenticable because any network node can evaluate it and determine that it was signed by the publisher's key. The authentication mechanism can vary significantly between different sets of publishers and users, allowing computational resources to be used according to specific needs of various application scenarios. The computational load can also be spread among several authentication packets, even though CCN packets are designed to be individually authenticable. The validation of the name–content binding is simply syntactic, that is it validates that the key was indeed used to sign the content, not imposing any meaning to it as property or as a key trust criterion.

The architecture proposed by CCN is the basis for the development of the Named Data Networking (NDN) project [ZHA 10]. This project aims to develop the required concepts that complement CCN to allow full adoption of ICNs. Issues such as global content routing, efficient name-based routing, content-based applications development, security and privacy features, among others, are part of the research agenda of the project. NDN has a deployed testbed with more than 11 nodes, located in leading research centers in the United States. Users connect to this testbed via User Datagram Protocol (UDP) tunnels, extending the CCN-based network to their campus and home networks.

3.4. Publish-subscribe Internet routing paradigm/ publish-subscribe Internet technologies

The Publish-Subscribe Internet Routing Paradigm (PSIRP) [LAG 10] architecture, in contrast to other ICN proposals, specifies a content-oriented architecture without employing existing connectivity and data transfer technologies such as TCP/IP. Heavily based on publish/subscribe networks concepts, PSIRP defines publications, or contents, as associations between persistent identifiers and data to be published. Self-certifiable names are bound to content and are of the form of cryptographic hashes.

PSIRP uses the *rendezvous*[1] [VIS 09] concept to resolve content names. Publishers announce their content in local *rendezvous* networks, which perform the association between data sources and subscribers whenever a specific content is requested. Scope Identifiers (S_{id}) are issued by publisher nodes, which are content-oriented identifiers that allow content distribution by other data sources. Data sources are nodes that cache content at the edge of the network and use the *rendezvous* system to announce their *Rendezvous* Identifiers (R_{id}). All content must be requested through the use of dual identifiers: S_{id}, which provides the logical content identification and its allowed data sources, and R_{id}, which provides possible data sources from a specific scope, fully specifying the desired publication request. S_{id} and R_{id} both use pairs of flat identifiers of the form "P:L", where P is the public key of the owner of the scope namespace and L is an arbitrary label of the publication. Local *rendezvous* networks are interconnected by a *rendezvous* interconnection (RI), a hierarchical DHT present in all PSIRP architectural domains, which even allows S_{id} and R_{id} translations to exterior networks' domains.

Publication $_{id}$ resolution returns an indication of branching nodes (BN) belonging to the distribution tree of that publication. The subscription is then routed through the various PSIRP domains, being forwarded to specific BNs as shown in Figure 3.3. The routing system is responsible for gathering and maintaining information of the delivery tree of each scope, besides caching popular content in the network. BNs select routes for new subscriptions based on network topology information and metrics derived from

---

1 French word for "encounter".

measurements of traffic intensity obtained by a topologically distributed management system. These nodes manage large caches and all delivery-tree branching (or interconnection) when there are multiple subscriptions to the same publication, similar to multicasting.

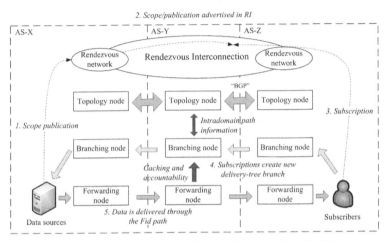

Figure 3.3. *PSIRP simplified architecture [LAG 10]*

The forwarding system [JOK 09] is responsible for the publication delivery to subscribers. By deploying efficient delivery trees, forwarding nodes (FN) deliver packets through interfaces belonging to the distribution tree of a given publication, identified by a Forwarding Identifier (F_{id}). F_{id}s are Bloom filter-based identifiers that allow FNs to forward packets through source routes. Since all links have an identification, the Link Identifier (Link ID), which is also represented by a Bloom filter, it is possible to encode the delivery tree in a Bloom filter and use it as the F_{id}. Each FN taking part in the delivery tree has only to perform a simple logical AND operation between the Link ID and the F_{id} of the packet header to check whether its interfaces belong to the delivery tree. If the result of this AND is the Link ID itself, that interface belongs to the delivery tree of that content and must forward the packet. This mechanism is subject to false positives since it employs Bloom filters for encoding information. When used for identifying interfaces, Bloom filters may cause the AND operation to lead to false positives, causing sending the packet to an unwanted interface, not a branch of the delivery tree. An example of this mechanism is illustrated in Figure 3.4.

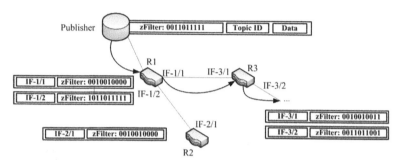

Figure 3.4. *An example of PSIRP forwarding [JOK 09]*

Built over the foundations raised by the PSIRP architecture proposal, the Publish/Subscribe Internet Technologies (PURSUIT) Project [FOT 10] was created in order to research and develop PSIRP's concepts. Mobility, privacy, network storage and accountability issues are among research areas of the project. One of the major goals of the PURSUIT project is the development of solutions and mechanisms for the innovative services creation and delivery, leveraging the full potential of these new information structures. Algorithmic content identification is one of the concepts explored in PURSUIT, as well as applying new content fragmentation and efficient distributed storage mechanisms. The nature of PURSUIT architecture, hierarchical and recursive, allows nodes to natively manage mobility by handling scopes, transparent to the network core. Thus, supporting mobility is one of the topics of interest in the project development. Mechanisms for authentication and accounting require extensions to support PURSUIT systems.

Issues related to topology management, routing and forwarding on all levels of the architecture require the development of a comprehensive management platform. The PURSUIT project has a testbed with dedicated servers located in various American and European research institutes, corresponding to more than 25 PURSUIT nodes spread in an intercontinental content network.

3.5. Content-centric inter-network architecture

Content-centric inter-network (CONET) architecture [DET 11] proposes a new CONET layer that provides users with network access to remote named-resources rather than to remote hosts. In CONET, named-resources can be data, as seen in other architectures, or service access points, both identified by a unique network identifier (NID). CONET focuses on the local support of in-network caching functionality to deploy a stateless yet efficient name-based routing supported by the interest/data tuple, borrowed from [JAC 09a], which can be integrated into legacy IP networks or applied in traditional clean-slate or overlay deployment approaches.

The CONET architecture aims to interconnect numerous CONET Sub Systems (CSS), which can take many forms: nodes directly connected by a point-to-point link, such as Point-to-Point Protocol (PPP) or an UDP/IP overlay link, or layer 2/layer 3 networks, such as Ethernet or IPv4/IPv6 networks. This basic idea gives CONET scalability to be deployed over the point-to-point links, IP Autonomous Systems or even the whole Internet. To be able to provide such a feature, CONET splits the network stack into two blocks: the CONET and the under-CONET layers. The CONET layer treats content as a first-class citizen, while the under-CONET layer simply connects nodes or CSSs. A CSS is deployed by a number of CONET nodes and uses an under-CONET mechanism to allow data flow among them.

Each node has a CSS address, which is consistent with the traversed under-CONET technology, such as an Ethernet MAC address or IPv4 address. Similar to the mechanism presented in section 3.3, CONET nodes obtain wanted content by issuing requests, named interest CONET Information Units (CIUs), receiving named data CIUs in response. Those data CIUs carry content chunks and can be forwarded toward the requester and cached for future use. CONET nodes are named after their function in a CSS: end-nodes (EN) request content by issuing interest CIUs; serving-nodes (SN) store, advertise and provide content; border-nodes (BN) connect different CSSs, forwarding interests and data CIUs between them and also act as cache for data CIUs; internal-nodes (IN) are optional and act inside a CSS to provide in-network caches; and optional name-system-nodes (NS) are used in the CSS name-based routing. An example of inter-networked CSSs and of node functionality can be found in section 3.5. All content, be it data or a named service, is identified by a NID. A NID is defined by a tuple of the form <namespace ID, name>, in which the namespace ID determines the naming conventions for the requested name, setting its own rules for content name publishing. Thus, each name declared in the name field represents a uniquely defined namespace-specific content name. Names are flat, as presented in section 3.2, also of the form P:L. The name-based routing, as will be presented next, singles out the CSS address associated with the requested NID.

As previously cited, the CONET layer is based on a TCP-like approach, similar to [JAC 09a]. An EN requests data by issuing an interest CIU for a certain NID, which is encapsulated in a carrier-packet and forwarded according to the CONET name-based routing. This routing process singles out the CSS address of the next node toward the most suitable node holding the requested data, allowing nodes to properly forward it. Differently from CCN's breadcrumbs,

CONET nodes do not store network state information. The EN CSS address and the set of CSS addresses of the traversed interfaces are appended in the carrier-packet in a path-info control field, allowing data to flow toward EN based on source routing. So, the first in-path CONET node able to provide the requested data, which could be a BN, an IN or an SN, responds to the request by issuing a data CIU. The encapsulated CIU traverses the same CSSs of the request, in the downward direction, and may be cached by any BN or IN along the path. This process repeats in each of the traversed CSSs, where the under-CONET mechanism, like IP, is responsible for routing the packet toward the EN. The name-based routing scheme, the lookup-and-cache routing, uses a fixed number of entries in its routing tables as a route cache. In case there is a miss in a route lookup, the node looks up the wanted route entry for a name in a name-system-node. NSs act as DNS, which holds route entries for a single CSS, serving one specific namespace. In case the SN is in the same CSS as the NS, the route entry corresponds to the CSS address of the SN; on the contrary, the entry is the CSS address of a BN. From the BN to the next CSS, the CIUs are routed according to whatever technology lies under the information-centric layer, such as the under-CONET mechanism.

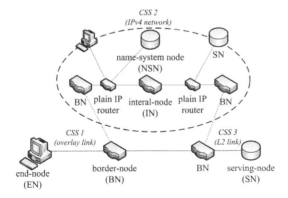

Figure 3.5. *CONET architecture example [DET 11]*

CONET differs considerably from other proposed architectures in respect of its alleged deployment flexibility. The clean-slate approach or overlay approach, as seen in DONA, PSIRP and other proposals, is also possible, but what makes CONET so flexible is the integration approach proposed in [DET 11]. A new IPv4 option is created, called the CONET Option [DET 12a], in order to allow IP-CONET integrated networks. In this kind of integration, BNs and INs could be IP routers with extended CONET functionality. Thus, the fast-forwarding path of routers could be used for both IP packets and CONET carrier-packets forwarding operations, with IP and name-based routing tables. Since CONET can be deployed over so many different scenarios, it is possible to extend it to cover the whole Internet or a set of IPv4 CSSs, possibly Autonomous System CSSs, integrated under CONET. The clear disadvantage of this integration mechanism is the new IP option, which in turn is less disruptive than the clean-slate approach.

3.6. Other architectures

Besides the already presented architectures, there are also other proposals for ICN implementation. TRIAD [CHE 00], NetInf [AHL 08] and Multicache [KAT 11], to name a few. TRIAD was the first work to propose a content-based communication architecture using URLs in HTTP requests as the content name. TRIAD performs redirection of requests to closest copies, in a CDN-like closest replica fetching, requiring storage capability and an information-centric layer in all routers. NetInf, an architecture proposed by the 4WARD[2] project, uses some concepts that are also presented in DONA and PSIRP/PURSUIT: flat names and DHT-based routing, most precisely. NetInf allows the use of persistent identifiers, as presented in section 4.1, and the separation

---

2 Available at http://www.4ward-project.eu/.

between publication and data, allowing the coexistence of multiple versions of the same publication. Multi-cache explores the multicast communication primitive for content distribution, implementing a Pastry-based [ROW 01] overlay network for content caching, replica location and content delivery itself.

3.7. General comparison

The comparison in Table 3.1 shows the main features of each of the already presented architectures. CBN, for its use of AVP naming, allows nodes to search the network for specific content and subscription of *a priori* unpublished content. However, AVPs can refer from none to all possible attributes for content identification, severely burdening route tables (of the order of 2^A, where A is the total number of attributes). In addition, any change to predicates that are not covered (or aggregated) by other predicates needs to be disseminated throughout the network, having great impact over the amount of local control traffic.

Characteristic	CBN	DONA	CCN/NDN	PSIRP/PURSUIT	CONET
Flat naming		X		X	X
Hierarchical naming			X		
AVP naming	X				
Structured routing		X		X	
Unstructured routing	X		X	X	
In-network caching		X	X	X	X
Content security		X		X	

Table 3.1. *General comparison*

DONA, in turn, uses flat content names, which grant persistence and uniqueness to identifiers. Owing to the architectural usage of hierarchical routing, which defines systematic and centralized flows of routing information and data, the impact of control traffic on the network is not likely to be significant. The use of non-aggregatable identifiers, however, leads to the use of a single entry per content in the routing tables, representing a critical point with respect to scalability of the architecture.

CCN/NDN are based on hierarchical naming, allowing names to be aggregated. The interest diffusion mechanism, however, has a significant impact on the amount of control traffic in the network. The use of in-network cache also ends up storing content closer to the network edge, adding even more complexity to the process of route aggregation. By adopting design principles similar to those of TCP/IP and CCN/NDN, this allows the adoption of legacy and well-proven mechanisms for content delivery, granting a gradual adoption and eventual replacement of the previous technology.

PSIRP/PURSUIT, similar to DONA, identify their content with flat identifiers, leading to the same persistence and uniqueness found in DONA. The structure of the hierarchical-DHT *rendezvous* system enables load distribution among all participating domains, normalizing the computational requirements of the network nodes. By totally breaking with TCP/IP concepts, PSIRP/PURSUIT establish a clean-slate architecture, hindering its adoption on a global scale.

CONET mixes some of the concepts introduced by DONA, CCN and PSIRP to present a very flexible ICN architecture. Whether deployed as a clean-slate network, an overlay system or in interoperation with legacy technology, CONET provides access to named-resources. CONET nodes only store a small subset of the routing entries locally, provided there is a name-system to cache route-by-name entries.

4

Challenges

The research on ICN, although quite recent, has already experienced some progress with a large number of propositions and solutions covering a wide range of problems and challenges for different issues. However, there are still many open problems and practical aspects for deployment that call for a more detailed investigation. This chapter discusses the main challenges related to naming, routing, caching, security, economic models, practical aspects for deployment and real-time applications. For each subject, we present the main contributions in the literature and try to point out some possible future directions.

4.1. Naming

Content names are the basic network primitive of all architectures proposed to ICNs, as discussed in Chapter 3. In fact, the naming mechanism adopted by each architecture provides different levels of persistence, scalability and user-friendliness. Ideally, an ICN architecture should provide globally unique, secure, location-independent and human-friendly names [BAR 12]. Thus, the main challenge in this area is to develop a naming mechanism that fulfills all these requirements. In practice, the current naming approaches – flat, hierarchical, and attribute-value based – partially satisfy a few of them [CHO 11].

Flat naming approaches provide uniqueness but suffer from lack of hierarchy and, thus, flat names are difficult to aggregate. Consequently, network scalability may be compromised because of the size of the routing tables. Ghodsi *et al.* [GHO 11b], however, argue that flat naming does not prevent explicit aggregation of names. To prove this, they propose an aggregation scheme based on self-certifying names employed by DONA. Basically, aggregatable identifiers are generated by concatenating individual flat names. This explicit aggregation is possible because names used by DONA are unique and have the aforementioned format P:L. In this case, content names have the following format: $name_1.name_2.name_3...name_n$, wherein each component $name_i$ is an individual and unique flat name. The authors called this structure aggregation invariant. The key idea is that when a node is looking for routing entries for $name_1$, it will probably find one entry for $name_2$; and when the node is doing the same for $name_2$, it will find entries for $name_3$ and so on. Another important remark is that no changes are required in routing tables. Routing entries are still composed of individual names and their associated outgoing port. However, when a router deals with a concatenated name, it searches for the deepest match and then forwards data based on the entry found. In deepest match, a router is looking for an exact match for each individual name that composes the concatenation. For example, if a router is looking for entries related to the concatenated name X.Y.Z – where X, Y and Z are the individual names – it starts the deepest match procedure from the end of the concatenated name (Z) and continues name-by-name toward the beginning (X), until a match or a not-found answer. According to the authors, deepest match has two advantages over longest prefix match. They argue that, first, the searching algorithm is simpler to implement and, second, the aggregation procedure is performed only by the naming mechanism and thus changes in the routing mechanism are not needed. Similarly to the hierarchical names, the concatenation of flat names can be used for representing structured content. In the previous example, X might represent the entire set of contents of a particular publisher, Y might be one large file of this set and Z might be a particular chunk of this file. In this case, explicit aggregation provides a "virtual hierarchy" to the flat naming approach. The authors also argue that virtual hierarchy aggregation is more flexible than a strict hierarchy because it allows different forms of aggregation involving the same name to coexist at the same time. For example, name X can be part of a large number of different concatenations, such as W.V.X and Y.Z.X, which increases the probability of finding routing entries to it. In contrast, hierarchical names are aggregated only to prefix within a higher level in the hierarchy. For example, a name like br.uff.classes is only related to aggregates br and br.uff.

Li *et al.* [LI 12] also experimentally evaluate the scalability of naming mechanisms, in particular, the CCN hierarchical naming mechanism. Details about this work are presented in section 5.2.

Hierarchical naming mechanisms provide aggregation. Consequently, these mechanisms are considered scalable because they reduce the number of entries in routing tables and their update time. In addition, prefixes are unique. This fact allows content routers to use the longest prefix matching algorithm to forward contents, similar to what IP routers do on the current Internet. On the other hand, the same aggregation capacity – that provides scalability – compromises content persistence. Hierarchical names carry content properties explicitly. One change in the hierarchy, due to ownership transfer or publisher modification, for example, changes the content name. Thus, the challenge is to develop hierarchical mechanisms that provide persistence. For this reason, Bari *et al.* [BAR 12] argue that the most suitable approach is to adopt self-certifying flat names because they intrinsically provide persistence and also authenticity and uniqueness. However, a set of user-friendly keywords must be assigned to names. These keywords allow users to search the content through search engines.

Persistence can be also a problem to flat naming approaches, in particular, for mechanisms that employ names in the format P : L, as described in section 2.1.1. In this case, the publisher's public key is used to generate the content name and, consequently, this name is related to the content owner. If the publisher changes, the name also changes because a new name must be generated based on the public key of the new publisher. An alternative to solve this problem is employed by the NetInf architecture [DAN 10]. Dannewitz *et al.* decouple the content name from the content ownership by adopting two different approaches. First, they consider a public key PK_{IO}, which is associated with the content itself and not with a specific publisher. Thus, the content name is given by PK_{IO} : L. In the case of owner change, the previous owner must send the private key SK_{IO} to the new owner through a secure channel. After that, the new owner is able to sign the content using the same key. The second approach generates a new pair of public–private keys at every owner change but it does not modify the original content name. Basically, the new owner uses its own private key, SK_{latest}, to sign the content and inserts this signature as metadata in packets. The *hash* of the original public key PK_{IO} remains unchanged in the content name. In addition, the pair $PK_{\text{latest}}/SK_{\text{latest}}$ is authorized by the original pair PK_{IO}/SK_{IO} by using a certificate chain [CLA 01].

Flat names are also not (or less) human-friendly. Thus, flat naming approaches require external mechanisms to map content names to human-friendly identifiers, such as search engines and recommendation systems [KOP 07]. Basically, name resolution has two steps: (1) a content name is resolved to a single or a set of locators, and after that (2) the content request is routed toward one of the retrieved locators [BAR 12].

D'Ambrosio *et al.* [D'AM 11] propose a hierarchical name-resolution service called Multi-level Distributed Hash Table (MDHT). The authors argue that existing name-resolution systems, such as DNS and common DHTs, do not provide low latency and efficient network utilization for an expected namespace with 10^{15} identifiers. This is an estimation to implement ICNs at the Internet scale. MDHT, on the other hand, is a scalable solution for global name-resolution considering non-hierarchical namespaces. With MDHT, contents are retrieved based on a two-step process similar to other name resolution systems. First, the name is resolved into a list of locators that indicates copies of the desired content. This step is referred to as the resolution phase. In the next step, called the content forwarding phase, a set of locators is selected from the list according to network conditions, for example. After that, content is sent by one or multiple sources to the requester. The resolution phase is the core of the MDHT system. In order to store name-locator bindings, MDHT employs multiple interconnected DHT systems, called DHT areas. Each DHT area represents a network on a different topological level. Basically, three levels are considered: the Autonomous System (AS), the Point of Presence (POP) and the Access Node (AN) levels. The different areas are arranged in such way to reflect the underlying network topology. The AN level, for example, is the lowest level and these nodes work similarly to a local DNS server, that is ANs receive name requests directly from clients. ANs also use a local hash table. Each area can employ its own DHT mechanism, such as Pastry and Chord, for example. Furthermore, each MDHT node participates in its own DHT area and in some or all higher level areas. Consequently, these higher level areas aggregate the nodes of the lower level areas into a single and larger area. For this reason, authors call this structure the nested hierarchical approach. Routing and forwarding requests are performed in two different levels. First, intra-area routing/forwarding is performed by using the DHT mechanism chosen by the area. Inter-area routing/forwarding is performed through the MDHT nodes that belong to both respective levels. The authors also argue that the nested hierarchical approach makes deployment of the MDHT system easy because it can be deployed in small networks first and, after that, these small networks can be interconnected to build a larger system. The MDHT system is not restricted to a specific ICN architecture. It can be used by any approach that requires a name-resolution system. Preliminary results show that an MDHT system can scale to the Internet level, that is MDHT is able to manage 10^{15} objects considering the current storage technology and 1/10th of the DNS nodes currently running.

Liu *et al.* [LIU 12] also propose a name-resolution mechanism based on multi-level DHT, called Scalable Multi-level Virtual Distributed Hash Table (SMVDHT). Basically, this approach combines name aggregation and multi-level virtual DHTs to achieve scalability by reducing the size and the update overhead of name-resolution tables. To do this, authors use underlying intra- and inter-domain IP routing protocols to build multilevel virtual DHTs, which are more efficient than conventional hierarchical DHT schemes and also simplify network management.

In contrast, Zhang *et al.* [ZHA 10] aim at avoiding external resolution mechanisms. The key idea is to use hierarchical names assigned by ISPs, which is very similar to the assignment of IP addresses, but without limiting the size of identifiers. Thus, a content published by a particular user that uses a given service provider could be named `/provider/users/user/content`. In fact, this approach makes the server provider management easier and increases the potential of route aggregation, but tends to associate identifiers with content locations.

Sollins [SOL 12] introduces one more property to contents: pervasiveness. The idea is that content should be spread everywhere to increase availability and distribution efficiency. She argues that persistence and pervasiveness are basic requirements for any naming mechanism for ICNs and thus introduces the Pervasive Persistent Identification System (PPInS). The proposed system defines three different layers: the user application, the PPInS and the ICN layers. The first layer is composed of a set of mechanisms that support human-friendly identification, for example search engines, references embedded in books, among others. Thus, users are able to request contents easily. The PPInS layer basically resolves the name given by the top layer into an ICN identifier depending on the bottom layer. For example, if the ICN layer is PURSUIT, the PPInS provides an RID; in case of CCN, it returns a CCN hierarchical name. This is the main advantage of PPInS: it allows multiple resolutions services for different namespaces running simultaneously.

Different applications may also require different naming approaches. Wang *et al.* [WAN 12a], for example, introduce a naming mechanism specific for vehicular applications that runs on vehicle-to-vehicle (V2V) networks. The user case considered is the dissemination of traffic information and the mechanism proposed is based on CCN architecture. The authors aim at introducing a naming mechanism that allows publishers to describe precisely what content they have to offer and users to express clearly what content they want. They conclude that the following structure /traffic/ geolocation/timestamp/data_type/nonce is general enough to allow users to request traffic data surrounding a specific geographical area or a period of time and receive accurate data. Security, however, as discussed in section 4.4, is still an open problem.

Recently, several studies proposed modifications on HTTP to allow seamless deployment of ICNs alongside the current Internet architecture [SAR 12, WAN 12b, GHO 11a, POP 10]. The naming mechanism in these proposals has a key role because all content-centric caching and routing operations are based on identifiers introduced in HTTP. Sarolahti *et al.* [SAR 12] propose an ICN architecture based on using information-centric HTTP proxies, called ICN-HTTP. Different from most clean-slate architectures for ICNs, ICN-HTTP keeps the backward compatibility with the existing HTTP-based infrastructure, that is servers, proxies and Web browsers. The key idea is to make HTTP a location-independent protocol. To achieve this goal, a new secure self-certifying identifier is introduced in the HTTP header in a field called Secure-Name[1]. This identifier uses the same structure P:L adopted by DONA, except that with HTTP it is possible to use variable-length strings as the content label. The secure self-certifying identifier is carried by an HTTP request and thus information-centric HTTP proxies can route the requests based on the Secure-Name field. In this context, the HTTP request is similar to a CCN interest packet. ICN-HTTP proxies can also cache the HTTP responses that were requested using the secure name. Thus, ICN-HTTP proxies build an overlay network to distribute content on top of the IP network. These proxies do not need public IP addresses because HTTP (content) requests are routed according to secure names. In fact, proxies must only be connected to neighbors and thus they need its IP addresses. Users should not have access and manipulate the secure name directly. The authors propose that the HTTP

---

1 The main reason to introduce the secure name in the HTTP header rather than replace URL is to keep backward compatibility.

client user interface is responsible to map and present the secure name to the user in a friendly format. DNS can be used to translate user-friendly names into secure names but it is not mandatory.

Wang *et al.* [WAN 12b] follow the same direction of the previous proposal. They propose to run HTTP on CCN architecture and thus introduce the concept of a HTTP-CCN gateway. The role of this gateway is to map HTTP request and HTTP response into CCN interest and data packets, respectively. The main goal of this proposal is to develop a CCN test bed that runs with real HTTP traffic. Thus, authors intend to find a transitional way that is attractive mainly to service providers. Instead of including a new field in the HTTP header, Wang *et al.* modify the URL by adding a prefix that indicates the routing information needed by the CCN router. For example, the URL `http://www.ic.uff.br` changes to `ccnx:/default/GET/http/www.ic.uff.br` and thus we have the name of the corresponding interest. The new interest name includes both the protocol component `http` and the HTTP method component `GET`. Modified URLs can also indicate a specific gateway rather than the default.

There is a consensus about the properties that content names should have: global uniqueness, security, location independent and human-friendly. In practice, there is no single mechanism that satisfies these requirements, as corroborated by the discussion in this section. There is no formal proof but Smetters and Jacobson [SME 09] argue that a naming mechanism might satisfy up to two of the aforementioned properties simultaneously. In addition, there is no consensus on which approach presents more advantages. The network requires, for example, a secure and efficient method to verify the content provenance. Users, on the other hand, are interested in retrieving the content by using human-friendly names that do not satisfy network requirements. Therefore, naming mechanisms for ICNs are still an important challenge to be investigated.

4.2. Routing

The goal of ICN routing mechanisms is to locate one of the multiple copies of the content that are distributed on the network. Similarly to naming mechanisms, routing mechanisms for ICN have several desired properties as listed by Bari *et al.* [BAR 12]: scalability, content state, discovery of closest copy, resolution and retrieval locality, discovery guarantee, network-level deployment and security infrastructure. No single mechanism provides all of them. In fact, it is difficult to provide even a few of them simultaneously.

Several studies have already analyzed the scalability of name-based routing mechanisms, such as TRIAD [CHE 00], ROFL [CAE 06] and pub/sub systems [MAR 10]. Scalability of ICN routing mechanisms, however, is more challenging to provide because of two characteristics of these networks: the expected size of routing tables and the difficulty to aggregate names. According to Bari *et al.* [BAR 12], the biggest Border Gateway Protocol (BGP) *table* found today has 4×10^5 routes that cover 3.8×10^9 and 6×10^8 hosts. On the other hand, Google has indexed approximately 10^{12} URLs. Thus, the name-based routing mechanisms employed by ICNs must deal with an expected namespace of several orders of magnitude higher than the current address space. To achieve scalability, the current Internet routing protocols generally employ hierarchical structures based on location-dependent identifiers. BGP, for example, employs prefix-based routing and route aggregation to reduce by a factor of 10^4 the number of routes necessary to cover all IP addresses in use. However, it is difficult to aggregate names in ICNs depending on the naming approach adopted by an ICN architecture. Alternatively, hierarchical structures must be defined based on names, similar to the name-resolution systems presented in section 4.1, or protocols should employ techniques to disseminate messages to all nodes. Flooding is a simple and stateless approach which can do this but may lead to high control overhead depending on the network size. In this case, scalability is compromised.

In order to reduce the overhead, routers can use only local information to disseminate messages, that is information from direct neighbors and its own [ZHA 10]. Rosensweig and Kurose [ROS 09] introduce Best Effort CONtent Search (BECONS), which is a query routing policy. In this approach, requests for a file are routed initially toward its source rather than disseminated to all nodes. BECONS employs a probabilistic approach based on breadcrumbs, which are volatile data structures used to store information about content received and forwarded in each router. This approach works as follows. Suppose that a router recently received and forwarded a given content and now it receives a new request for this same content but it was already removed from the cache. In this case, the router should forward this new request to the source (the upstream router) or to the user served (downstream router) in order to increase the probability of finding a copy of the desired content. This probability also depends on the caching policy adopted. The authors show that policies such as Least Recently Used (LRU) and downstream forwarding provide higher gains because, in this case, routers store most recent content for more time. Consequently, it increases the cache hit and the probability of responding to the content request. A discussion about caching policies is presented in section 4.3.

Lee *et al.* [LEE 11] also introduce a similar approach called Scalable Content Routing for Content-Aware Networking (SCAN). With SCAN, only neighbors exchange routing messages periodically. Thus, when a router receives a request, it forwards this message only to the neighbors that are able to forward or to answer it. This procedure is called scan routing. Information about neighbors is derived from the content routing table (CRT), which is a compact structure for storing information relating to the content stored in each node. As the number of entries in the routing table can grow considerably in ICNs, SCAN compresses the information using Bloom filters [BRO 03]. Bloom filters are data structures that allow us to verify whether a particular element is a member of a given set. A Bloom filter is usually formed by an array of m bits, all initially filled with 0. To insert an element e_1 in the filter, we must apply k-independent hash functions $(h_i(e_1))$. Each hash function $(h_i(\cdot), i \in \mathbb{N} | 1 \leq i \leq k)$ returns an integer in the interval $[0, m-1]$, which is an index to the array of bits. Thus, the bits corresponding to the result of each hash function $h_i(\cdot)$ are set to 1. To verify whether a given element belongs to the set, we must simply compute the value for the k hash functions with this element, and then check if all the k resulting bits are set to 1 (or, in the case of accepting approximations, if at least a certain number of bits are set to 1) [LEE 11]. It should be noted that results from Bloom filters are probabilistic, and thus they are subject to false positives, that is considering an element as a member of the set even though it has never been inserted. In terms of its application in ICN routing, it implies sending data to the wrong neighbors, which can significantly increase the control overhead. Therefore, for distributed applications, like the one mentioned above, it is important to consider different versions of Bloom filters that address the false positive rate problem [LAU 11, MOR 12]. Bloom filters are also used for representation of predicates in pub/sub systems [CAR 09].

Several approaches, as described in section 4.1, employ hierarchical structures and circular DHTs to resolve names in locators. Remember that names are not location dependent. Thus, overlays are built not based on metrics such as distance or delay but based on relations between names. This is a problem for routing algorithms that may suffer with the route-stretch problem, that is routes computed are not the shortest path in terms of proximity. Consequently, applications may experience longer delays. To avoid this problem, mechanisms that take into account the physical proximity to route requests or to select neighbors in the overlay must be employed [RAT 02]. Both mechanisms – proximity-based routing or proximity-based neighbor selection – are already employed by protocols for P2P systems. CAN [RAT 01] and Chord [STO 03], two of the most cited protocols to build P2P overlays, employ proximity-based routing. With CAN, nodes periodically measure the RTT to their neighbors. With Chord, nodes maintain a list of closest nodes – ordered by RTT – that must be used to reach a given region. On the other hand, Pastry [ROW 01], another protocol to build P2P overlays, selects neighbors based on the number of hops, RTT or throughput. The multi-cache [KAT 11] introduces an overlay architecture for ICN, which implements Pastry as a routing substrate.

Eum *et al.* [EUM 12] propose the Potential-Based Routing (PBR): a routing mechanism that provides availability, adaptability, diversity and robustness to ICNs. The proposed protocol is based on the same idea introduced by the directed diffusion protocol for wireless sensor networks [INT 03]. The basic idea is to define the potential field on the network and then route packets toward the direction of maximum force. PBR operates in the following way. First, it divides nodes into two groups: caching nodes n_c and non-caching nodes n_{nc}. A caching node has a content stored in its cache. After that, the potential value at each caching node is calculated based on the quality of the content provided by this node to a given node n. The content quality depends on the capacity of outgoing links and the processing power of n_c and also on the distance^2 between n and n_c. A caching node with high-capacity outgoing links or high processing power probably provides high-quality content. On the other hand, the quality decreases as the distance between nodes increases. Content requests are thus routed based on quality, that is, a request that arrives to node n is forwarded to a neighbor of n that maximizes the potential difference. Thus, requests are attracted to the best content providers – a caching node or a repository – in terms of quality. According to the authors, PBR achieves availability because requests are forwarded not only to the repository but also to caching nodes. This is the expected behavior of most ICN architectures. Contents on caching nodes are added and removed dynamically, which changes the potential values at each node. Thus, PBR provides adaptability by considering this volatile behavior to forward requests. Diversity is provided by PBR because this protocol takes quality into account during the request forwarding process rather than only considering the proximity. The PBR protocol is also robust against a single point failure because it executes it in a fully distributed manner. The authors combine the PBR protocol and a random caching policy and propose a new ICN architecture called the Cache Aware Target idenTification (CATT) [EUM 12].

Interdomain routing is another challenging issue that must be addressed by ICN architectures. BGP is the *de facto* Internet standard for this purpose and is based on policies rather than finding the shortest paths. DiBenedetto *et al.* [DIB 11] argue that ICN architectures should also consider a interdomain protocol similar to BGP. Actually, these architectures radically change police agreements because of two main reasons. First, administrators are able to define

_____

2 Distance means geographic proximity, number of hops, transmission delay or link cost.

policies with finer granularity based on content names rather than hosts. Second, in-network caching must be considered. Figure 4.1 illustrates the relations between ASes A, B, C and D. Relations among these are indicated by arrows (customer–provider relation) and lines (non-customer–provider relation). In these scenario, suppose C has downloaded a large popular video V through A and currently stores a copy of this video in its cache. Suppose that C and D also have an agreement to share content present in their own networks and also in the networks of their customers. This is the approach adopted today on the Internet. With ICN, on the other hand, C and D should also agree to share their caches and thus both reduce the amount of external content that they must have to download through their providers. In this case, D can retrieve the video V from C. It is also possible that C offers to its provider B the same video V stored in its cache and then pays less for the service offered by B. Thus, traffic engineering experiences new challenges in ICNs mainly because agreements are based on content names and caching capabilities. With this in mind, the authors define several policy parameters, in particular, for the CCN architecture and also present different use cases of these parameters. Basically, CCN allows network administrators to set control and data plane parameters rather than only control plane parameters as in BGP. It is possible to determine, for example, whether or not an incoming interest packet is allowed to access cached content, if a data packet must be cache or not and if an interest packet must be forwarded in all or just in a subset of faces depending on the sender of this packet – a customer or a peer. In summary, the authors aim at showing the economic incentives to ISPs considering that CCN is already deployed in practice.

Several desired properties of routing mechanisms are not currently addressed by any ICN architecture proposed.

Issues concerning the management of content state, for example, are not explored. Questions such as "How to update the metadata of a content?" and "How to delete a content?" are still undefined. Network-level deployment, discovery guarantees and security are also routing problems not investigated in depth by current approaches. The development of practical content routers is also under investigation. Chapter 5 presents, in more detail, the practical issues concerning content routers capabilities and constraints to operate in an information-centric network.

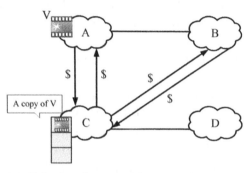

Figure 4.1. *Relations between ASes A, B, C and D and new agreements allowed by ICNs [DIB 11]. C receives the video V from A and stores V in this cache. After that, C can establish new agreements with B and D if both are interested to receive V*

4.3. Caching

One of the basic ideas of ICN is the universal storage of content on the network, which is accomplished by implementing *cache* in all routers in the network [GHO 11a]. The main goal is to improve the network performance for content distribution. This performance improvement is achieved by the reduction of the delay experienced by the user and a more efficient use of the bandwidth in the core of the network. Besides, the availability of multiple copies of the same content avoids a single point of failure. At last, the reduction of traffic near the content source reduces the processing load of the publisher.

Content storage and cache issues have been extensively studied, especially since the emergence of the *Web*. Recently, the use of CDNs also prompted a large number of works, mainly on the issue of distributing the caches in the network as well as allocating content into cache, to minimize the delay and optimize the use of the bandwidth in the network. However, the use of cache in information-oriented networks has quite different characteristics from those mentioned previously. The first important feature consists of implementing cache in all network components, forming a network of caches, also denominated in-network caching, as opposed to Web-caching, which presents a hierarchical tree topology, and CDNs, in which caches are placed at specific points in the network. This characteristic provides great flexibility for content allocation, enlarging access to this functionality to all network nodes and not only to the content servers, as it happens in CDNs. The second important feature is that in some ICN architectures, the content is divided into smaller pieces of the same size, named content chunks, and thus caches store chunks instead of storing the entire contents. Content size can have a significant impact on the performance of the content storage system [POD 03]. Therefore, in architectures such as CCN, using a fixed size for chunks simplifies the problem.

The main research topics in this area are: (1) analytical models for networks of caches, (2) replacement policies and (3) storage policies. All works in the literature present some kind of performance evaluation of the network of caches in order to investigate the proposed solutions. Therefore, the most commonly used metrics to measure the performance of networks caches are: (1) the hit ratio, which defines the fraction of content requests that were found in the cache,

(2) the delay perceived by the user, which measures the waiting time to receive a given content after sending its request and (3) the average number of hops a request goes through before being served. All studies use the Zipf-like distribution $(1/i^\alpha)$ to model the content popularity [BRE 99]. However, the studies use different values for the parameter α.

In the following section, we present the key challenges and proposed work on each of the research topics mentioned previously.

4.3.1. *Analytical models for networks of caches*

The major challenge in this research area is the significant complexity that represents a large-scale network of caches, like the size of the Internet. There are many studies that propose new models in an attempt to understand the dynamics and analyze the performance of networks caches [ROS 10, PSA 11, CAR 11a, CAR 11b, FRI 12]. There are some studies that model hierarchical Web-caching systems using specific topologies, in which the server content source is connected to the top of the hierarchy, as in tree topologies [CHE 01, CHE 02]. Furthermore, due to the complexity of these models, they are usually applied to small topologies, such as two-level trees [ROS 10].

In one of the first attempts to model networks of caches, Rosensweig *et al.* propose an approximate algorithm to characterize the behavior of networks caches with generic topologies [ROS 10]. Their approach is to define a single cache approximation for each router in the network. Thus, the requests arrival to this router is defined by the requests sent directly to the router, by a user, and the requests sent by neighbor routers, due to a cache miss, as illustrated in Figure 4.2. In the case of a cache miss, in which a given content is not found in the cache, the router forwards the request to the next hop in the shortest path to the content source. In a network of caches, using an iterative process, the algorithm updates the requests that arrive in each router until the entire network converges to a steady state. The authors claim that the proposed model is suitable for any topology regardless of scale. However, the complexity of the algorithm is given by $O(KB)$, which impairs the use of this model for networks with a large number of contents (K and large sizes of caches (B) [PSA 11].

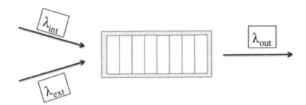

Figure 4.2. *A single cache approximation proposed in [ROS 10]*

To solve this problem, Psaras *et al.* [PSA 11] propose a simpler model for the cache of only one router. This model uses a continuous and homogeneous Markov chain, in which each state of the chain represents the current position of a content in the cache. The authors consider that whenever a content is requested, it is stored in the first position of the cache (top). In case of a content that is not in cache, all other contents are moved down one position. Otherwise, the requested content is moved to the top, and contents stored solely above the requested content change their position. Thus, considering a cache of size N, an element in the state $N + 1$ of the Markov chain is not in the cache. The model is also extended to a network of caches. The ultimate goal is to calculate the time that a content remains in cache. Finally, the authors extend the model for cascading two routers and analyze the performance of a network of caches with a tree topology.

Using a different approach, Carofiglio *et al.* [CAR 11b] proposed a model for transferring chunks in networks of caches. First, is proposed a probabilistic failure model when searching for a specific content (error probability) in a single router. The request process is modeled at two levels: content and chunk. The arrival process of requests is modeled using a Markov Modulated Rate Process (MMRP). Then, the authors extend the model to a network of caches with and without aggregation of requests, based on a binary tree topology and cascade topology. Finally, they present a closed-form expression for the mean stationary throughput with respect to several parameters, such as hit/miss ratio, content popularity, content size and cache size. In a second study, Carofiglio *et al.* [CAR 11a] extend the model previously proposed to consider limitations of bandwidth and storage capacity. Thus, the authors derive a closed-form expression for the average delivery delay of content considering these limitations added to the model.

In order to evaluate the impact of different types of traffic on the performance of a network of caches, Fricker *et al.* [FRI 12] model a tree-structured network of caches, considering four different types of content: *Web* objects, file sharing, user-generated content and video on demand. These categories have substantial different characteristics in terms of popularity, population size and content size. The model is based on an approximation of the performance of the dropping policies Least Recently Used (LRU) and Least Frequently Used (LFU) [CHE 02]. The authors show that the compromise between the cache size and the bandwidth used is strongly related to the characteristics of the stored content.

4.3.2. *Content replacement policies*

Packet replacement policies are associated with discarding contents whenever the cache reaches its maximum storage capacity and a new content, not yet stored in the cache, arrives. Therefore, a strategy to select what content will be discarded to make room for the last request is necessary. The two most used policies are LRU and LFU. The first, which is the simplest, discards the least recently accessed content while the second discards the content used less frequently. According to Podlipnig and Böszörmenyi [POD 03], although there is a significant amount of different policy proposals to content replacement, there is a strong argument claiming that the study of new more efficient policies is less important since the capacity of storage devices has shown a strong trend in growth, coupled with the constant decline in prices. Therefore, simple replacement policies present similar performances to more complex policies. However, for the networks of caches the reality is different. First, the cache size in routers is limited to relatively small amounts of storage capacity compared to the universe of contents to be stored, because of cost and performance [PER 11]. Therefore, it might be interesting to use a more efficient policy. Nevertheless, there is a trade-off between the complexity of the replacement policy and the processing capacity of a router. It means that routers cannot implement sophisticated and complex policies due to processing constraints. Therefore, most studies only analyze the performance of LRU and LFU policies, the latter being an upper limit to the speed of other policies [ROS 11a]. Still, many studies assess the performance of networks of caches considering different content replacement policies.

In one of the first attempts to investigate the performance of networks of caches, Choi et al. [CHO 09] evaluated through simulations two specific types of topology for content-oriented networks. In this work, the authors considered the tree topology and topology-based DHTs. They analyze the cache size, the transfer delay and the robustness to random failures of routers, in both topologies.

Rossini and Rossi [ROS 12] analyze the performance of networks of caches based on characteristics of the network structure. The authors consider several centrality metrics such as degree, closeness and betweenness, among others. These metrics reflect, in different ways, the importance of a node in the network. Thus, they use some real topologies with different structural characteristics. Finally, two criteria are proposed for defining the cache size for each network node, proportional to the centrality metrics. The most important result of this study shows that the impact of the topology metrics in defining different cache sizes is negligible, especially in relation to the complexity added by the proposed mechanism. In another work, Rossini and Rossi [ROS 11a] analyze the performance of networks of cache with different content discarding policies. Among the analyzed policies are LRU, FIFO, in which content stored first is discarded first, UNIF, where a content is chosen randomly with uniform distribution, and BIAS, in which two contents are randomly picked and the most popular is discarded. In a third study, Rossi and Rossini [ROS 11b], besides considering different discarding policies, the authors also consider locality models and forwarding strategies in the CCN architecture.

Carofiglio et al. [CAR 11c] present two new strategies for content discarding policies in order to provide quality of service. In the first strategy, the authors suggest the use of the technique of cache partitioning [LU 04], in which a fraction of the memory is allocated to each application. Because of the fact that the proposed allocation is static, the problem of cache underutilization arises whenever a particular application uses all its portion of the memory and starts using the discard policy, while there is still free memory space reserved for other applications. The second strategy consists of defining categories of priorities for applications. The key idea is to manage content discard based on these priorities, by choosing from which category a chunk will be discarded. In one of the proposed algorithms, a particular chunk can only be dropped to make room for another chunk of equal or higher priority.

An interesting alternative for LRU and FIFO policies consists of using a Time-To-Live-based policy (TTL) [FOF 12]. In this approach, each content stored in the cache is associated with a timer, namely, a TTL value. Thus, whenever a request for a given content arrives before its TTL expiration, the content can be retrieved, which represents a cache hit. However, when a request for a content arrives after the TTL expiration, there is a cache miss and the router should forward the request according to its routing table. The key idea for using the TTL-based approach is twofold: (1) it is a more general policy that can be configured to mimic the behavior of other replacement policies and (2) it is simpler to study analytically, since there is no fully successful attempt to model networks of LRU and FIFO caches, as seen in section 4.3.1.

4.3.3. *Content storage policies*

Content storage policies define which content should be stored in the cache. The policy commonly used in the literature consists of storing all new content indiscriminately. Rossi and Rossini [ROS 11a] evaluate the performance, through simulations, of different storage policies. The first is the policy of storing everything that arrives in the router with no discrimination. The second policy analyzed [ARI 10a] stores content randomly with a fixed probability p. The last policy evaluated is Leave a Copy Down (LCD), in which a content found in the cache of a given router, namely a cache hit, is only stored in the next router on the path to the user that has requested it [LAO 06]. The basic idea is to push popular content closer to the user, at the border routers. To implement this strategy, the one that responds to a given request, the publisher or a router in the delivery path, must mark the content packet to indicate to the next router in the way back that the packet must be stored. Then, when a router receives a data packet that is marked as "store", it must store the content in its cache and reset the *store bit*, which indicates it should not be stored by any other router in the delivery path. Thus, the first time a given content is requested, it travels along all the path to the origin and the publisher answers the request and marks the content packet as "store". The next router stores the packet. The second request for the same content will not arrive at the origin, because content will be returned by the $(r - 1)$ router in the delivery path, as illustrated in Figure 4.3.

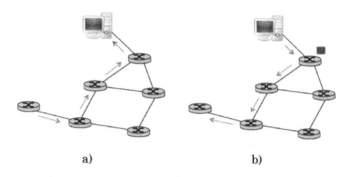

a)   b)

Figure 4.3. *Leave a copy down (LCD) scheme: a) The first request travels all the path and arrives at the origin due to consecutive cache misses; b) the publisher returns the content but only the first router in the wayback stores the content*

Another approach consists of defining content storage policies to provide a collaborative caching scheme. In this approach, caches cooperate with each other in order to improve the system performance. Several works have focused on this approach for traditional networks [LI 11, DAI 12, WOL 99, YAN 00]. However, designing a collaborative cache scheme for ICN is not a trivial task, since the communication overhead to assure the collaboration among content routers can be a real problem. Therefore, one of the main issues in employing collaborative caching in ICN lies in finding an efficient way to let content routers know what contents are stored in other routers. Cho *et al.* [CHO 12] propose a storage scheme in which the number of chunks stored depends on the contents popularity. Additionally, routers indicate to their neighbors if a given chunk should be stored or not by checking the storage bit. The goal is to avoid storing the same content in all nodes of the path. In this scheme, routers tend to push the most popular content in the direction of the routers closest to the users who have requested the content. Another attempt of applying collaborative caching in content-centric networks is presented in [GUO 12]. The key idea lies in coupling caching and forwarding decisions. The basic concept consists of building an Availability Information Base (AIB), which keeps information of the most popular content available in the cache of collaborative routers. Hence, in this proposal, each router must generate a popularity ranking sequence periodically with local information. Thus, content routers announce their sequence to the other routers, which must aggregate all the sequences received to form its own AIB. When a content request arrives, the router checks whether the content is stored in its cache. If yes, the router sends the content to the user. Otherwise, it must look for a corresponding entry in the pending table (PIT). If there is no entry in the PIT, then the router checks in its AIB if the content is available in another content router. Therefore, finding a collaborative router with the content of interest avoids forwarding the user request up to the content originator.

However, some authors argue that the concept of universal caching and collaborative caching, associated with simple replacement policies such as LRU, can represent a high cost without bringing enough performance improvement, mainly due to content popularity and the limited size of the cache [GHO 11a, CHA 12]. Therefore, the key idea is to employ a selective caching in which, solely, a subset of the nodes stores content in the cache. The simplest approach consists of selecting randomly one intermediate node along the delivery path. Chai *et al.* compares the performance of universal caching strategy to the random selective strategy, both using LRU. Results show as the selective strategy can present the same performance that the universal caching, especially in regular topologies like $k - ary$ trees. Then, they propose a centrality-based scheme, in which the caching decision is made upon the betweenness centrality of the node. The intermediate node in the delivery path with the highest betweenness centrality value is selected. Results show that this selective scheme outperforms the universal caching strategy, regardless of the topology, but shows a better result for scale-free topologies. In the same context of avoiding universal cache, Psaras *et al.* [PSA 12] propose a probabilistic storage policy in order to reduce cache redundancy, and as a consequence, improving the efficiency of available cache resources. The basic idea lies in predicting the cache capacity of a path of routers and the amount of traffic that passes through this path. The authors use these information to decide whether to store content in a specific router.

There is also research on new storage policies and cache placement in networks based on the paradigm *publishes/subscribes*. Diallo *et al.* [DIA 11] introduce new storage policies. The different policies prioritize different types of content, such as content that have a pending request and have already been expedited. The authors also analyze the performance of the proposed policies using different content discarding policies. Sourlas *et al.* [SOU 11] propose an algorithm to define the cache placement and the allocation of content replicas to enable access to contents which the publisher is no longer connected to the network.

Pacifici and Dan [PAC 13] argue that a future information-centric network is likely to be composed of autonomous systems (ASes), similar to the current Internet. It is clear that managing and dimensioning a large single cache network for optimal global performance is not feasible. Therefore, the ICN will be a network of cache networks, which is managed and optimized based on local performance. Thus, it is fundamental to understand the impact of the interaction between individual cache networks on the convergence and stability of the cache contents, and effects of the coordination between networks of caches. In one of the first attempts to address these issues, the authors consider a network of ASes, in which each AS maintains its own cache networks and establishes a content-level peering with other ASes [PAC 13]. The goal is to decrease their transit traffic costs. Then, the authors propose a model of the interaction and coordination between caches managed by peering ASes. Simulation results show that the content peering leads to stable content configurations, with or without coordination. The authors also investigate the effect of coordination on the cost efficiency and convergence speed.

4.4. Security

One of the main security issues in ICNs is trust in the content, namely in that when the user receives a certain content how to be sure it is actually the one that was requested. In the current Internet architecture, this problem is solved with the knowledge of the origin of the content and some characteristics of the communication. Knowledge of the origin implies trust in the search Website as well as in the DNS system [SME 09]. Therefore, there are three basic problems to be solved to provide trust in the content: (1) to verify the integrity of the document, (2) to verify the origin of the content and (3) to determine the relevance of the content obtained in relation to the requested one. Several works [KOP 07, WAL 04, POP 05] focus on solving these problems employing self-certifying names, where each name is generated through a cryptographic operation with the content itself. However, this approach generates a flat namespace, in which content lookup is substantially more complex than using DHT-based approaches. Furthermore, the self-certifying name approach only solves the integrity problem. Another approach is to perform a cryptographic operation with the key that was used to sign the content. This approach allows us to verify the origin of the content [POP 05]. However, the major problem of both techniques is the need for a mapping between the names generated from the hash functions and user-friendly names. This problem requires the existence of a mechanism that can provide trust in the mapping. To avoid this mapping, Koponen *et al.* [KOP 07] propose the concatenation of a label chosen by the content publisher, which is a user-friendly name, with the resulting hash function applied to the public key of the publisher. Nonetheless, the label is not signed, and thus allows an attacker to associate a valid content, and signed, to any label of its choice. Dannewitz *et al.* [DAN 10] have a similar approach for providing self-certifying names. Smetters and Jacobson [SME 09] proposed to authenticate the link between names and contents, rather than authenticating each link separately. Therefore, the purpose of names is restricted to content location and identification in a user-friendly manner. Authentication is achieved through validating the mapping between the content and its name.

Security is also a desirable property of names. Baugher *et al.* [BAU 12] proposed modifying the authentication method employed by CCN and DONA. Both architectures use digital signatures and symmetric key cryptography to verify content authenticity and integrity. In practice, this approach may compromise network scalability. CCN must bind a name to a public key and relies on a public key infrastructure (PKI) similar to Web browsers. On the other hand, DONA binds a self-certifying name to a real-world identity similarly to a public key repository. Therefore, to adopt CCN and DONA at the Internet scale, it needs to increase by three orders of magnitude the number of secure servers or the service rate of public key repositories, respectively [BAU 12]. Baugher *et al.* aim at increasing scalability by enschewing users to use public key cryptography to verify content authenticity and integrity. To do this, they introduce the concept of read-only data, which means contents that are already known before requested. Web pages, documents, music and video files are examples of read-only data. Data sent by streaming applications, for example, are not read-only. The authors also rely on two basic ideas: (1) read-only data can be announced to interested users before they request these data and (2) content name is given by the cryptographic hash of the content itself, which is called a self-verifying name. Different from self-certifying names used, for example, by DONA, self-verifying names do not need a public key to authenticate contents and symmetric key cryptography is optional to authenticate names. Content authenticity relies on cryptographic hashes of the requested content and not on digital signatures. Only the content name is signed. In practice, users have to access a catalog to get a self-verifying name for the content, which is signed by a notary. The role of the catalog is to map the hash name to a human-readable name. The notary has the legal authority to authenticate names. The disadvantage with this is that the content name might be transmitted through a secure out-of-band channel. Integrity is verified by applying the hash function to the content and checking the result with the content name.

Also regarding content naming, another important issue that is receiving attention is privacy. The basic principle of using content names to perform forwarding and routing tasks introduces security flaws in terms of user privacy. In ICNs, routers have direct access to the users content requests. Therefore, if the router is compromised, the attacker is able to monitor the requests submitted by the users and know exactly their interests. This approach allows not only for discovering user profiles but also for monitoring the user's daily life. For example, the attacker might know that a certain user will not be at home at the weekend just by capturing plane tickets the user has bought over the Internet. The lack of privacy also brings the censorship of content, a practice adopted by some countries, which is significantly facilitated by direct access to content request information. Lauinger *et al.* [LAU 12c] present different privacy attacks, as well as some countermeasures, and discusses the trade-off between privacy and performance. In order to hinder the work of the attackers to monitor content requests, Arianfar *et al.* [ARI 11] proposed a mechanism to increase users' privacy. The proposed scheme aims at preventing the identification of requests to prohibited contents, as well as the identification of prohibited content that was already retrieved. The technique consists of mixing blocks of prohibited content with normal content so that a chunk is composed of more than one block. Thus, the user must request a number of chunks to be able to recover more than one content, and not only the content of interest, which is forbidden. Thus, the attacker's job to find out what is being requested based only on chunk requests is quite difficult.

Another important problem of security in ICNs is the vulnerability to cache pollution attacks [GAO 06]. This attack consists of sending random requests for content in order to change content popularity, forcing routers to store unpopular contents in their caches. A more effective variation of this attack lies in only requesting unpopular contents. However, it requires prior knowledge of the content popularity. Finally, the most effective implementation of the cache pollution attack consists of requesting false contents, which are created by other attackers just to perform the attack. This way, caches are filled with contents that are outside the universe of valid contents. Xie *et al.* [XIE 12] propose a storage mechanism that reduces the effect of a cache pollution attack. The proposed mechanism stores only the most frequently requested contents. The authors show, through simulation, the efficiency of the proposed mechanism under a cache pollution attack, performed by sending random requests, uniformly distributed, to legitimate content.

Although security is an important research area, efforts to address the main problems are still quite limited and insufficient.

4.5. Mobility support in ICN

As previously cited, the identification and location decoupling made possible by the information-centric communication paradigm, provides ICNs with local mobility support. In this context, mobility is the ability of the network infrastructure to allow consumers and content providers to change their positions in the network topology without disruptions in existing content flows or unavailability of published content [TYS 12]. Traditional Internet architecture, based on the overloaded semantics of IP addresses, fails to cope with topological changes given it does not guarantee the preservation of ongoing connections in the presence of such changes. Solutions to this problem have been proposed, such as Mobile IP [JOH 04] and Host Identification Protocol (HIP) [MOS 08], but they do not directly address the content mobility issue since both solutions depend on topological information and on indirection points for traffic redirection. Different ICN architecture proposals address the mobility issue from different angles. Pioneer architectures presented some mobility-related gaps that have been fulfilled by subsequent architectures. For example, DONA uses out-of-band channels for content delivery such as TCP, which requires the re-establishment of end-to-end connections in face of node relocations, while CCN, in turn, approaches mobility locally through receiver-based control of the outstanding interests, resending requests in the case of failure, similar to the mechanism adopted by PSIRP.

The benefits related to the information-centric paradigm are numerous when it comes to mobility, both physical, when repositioning consumer and content provider nodes in the network; and logical, concerning the existence of multiple content copies. However, these benefits bring with them a number of research challenges, among them:

– *Opportunistic communication:* since all communication unfolds without any reference to node location, ICNs allow the exploration of the broadcast characteristic of the wireless medium. This principle enables the adoption of opportunistic mechanisms, widely exploited in Delay Tolerant Networks (DTNs). As data are transmitted without any reference to recipients, proactive storage, thereof, enables its later use, increasing content availability. Similarly, any node can satisfy the content request once in possession of a valid copy of the wanted data. However, dynamic content and intense node mobility can invalidate entries in routing tables and lead to outdated copies of content stored locally. Additionally, the adoption of broadcast communication can lead to a broadcast storm problem [NI 99], which must be dealt with within large, yet efficient, mobile network architectures. Large amounts of control traffic would be necessary to maintain network synchronization, which seems to be unfeasible in large network topologies.

– *Multipath content delivery:* the independence from both node location information and establishment of end-to-end connections enables ICNs to use multiple content providers simultaneously, exploring multiple paths in content delivery. The network layer must only deliver a valid copy of the wanted data to the application layer, regardless of which node sent it or what interface it was received on. This property reduces the load over the application layer due to mobility processes, which act transparently. However, the lack of end-to-end connections and independence from node location information turns preserving ongoing data flows into an issue in mobility scenarios, increasing the likelihood of discontinuities in these flows. Routing information aggregation, especially in hierarchical architectures, also shows an increase in complexity with multiple paths given the content dispersal within the network.

A direct result of the information-centric paradigm employment in mobility support, especially in wireless networks, is the potential data link layer overload in the presence of a large amount of content requests. The lack of binding between content identification and location precludes knowledge of end-to-end routes, which makes content delivery a complex problem to be solved. In these scenarios, a node can broadcast content requests without any specific destination, which can be answered by any node that receives a request and possesses a valid copy of the requested content. Information-centric architectures with broadcast-based communication primitives employ very simple receiver-driven forwarding mechanisms. The decision of relaying or not a previously received packet, based solely on local information, resides on each receiving node. A good example of this mechanism in ICNs was first presented in [MEI 10], introducing the Listen First Broadcast Later Protocol (LFBL).

LFBL nodes do not exchange any control information and store minimum information to allow forwarding decisions. This information, a distance metric associated with each registered content provider, is used by nodes to decide locally whether or not to rebroadcast packets. Whenever it receives information from the link layer, an LFBL node verifies this metric to determine its membership in an eligible forwarders group, similar to the anypath concept [LAU 12a, LAU 12b].

Every node, when broadcasting packets, inserts its own distance metric in relation to destination and source nodes in a cumulative and location-free way, using these metrics only in this decision process. Eligible nodes can rebroadcast the newly received packet, increasing the likelihood of a successful delivery. Determining itself as an eligible forwarder, the node then starts to sense the medium in search of a retransmission of the same packet during a variable time interval. This interval works as a back off timer and allows nodes to prioritize retransmissions with better distance metrics: the better the metric, the shorter the interval. If the node senses no retransmission within this interval, it can retransmit the packet; otherwise, it may be discarded since it has already been retransmitted. Wireless medium sensing and opportunistic usage of information are also employed in proactive in-network caching, allowing any content detected in the medium to be stored for future use. LFBL nodes can receive multiple contents in response to a single request, deciding for itself which of the responses answered its request properly.

Before LFBL, some other studies had addressed the optimization of broadcast communication in wireless networks. Packet rebroadcasting is used to circumvent the problems caused by frequent discontinuities typical of wireless architectures. Broadcast prioritization mechanisms grant a reduction in network resources utilization with little impact over the quality of packet delivery service. In [NAU 06], the Preferred Group Broadcasting (PGB) was proposed, a cross-layer prioritization mechanism that allows a node to determine its participation in the eligible forwarders group according to the received signal strength at the physical layer. The Dynamic Delayed Broadcasting (DDB) protocol, proposed in [HEI 06], also applies dynamic delayed forwarding (DFD) to reduce the network resources utilization. DDB nodes autonomously decide about packet retransmission using DFD functions with different objectives, such as hitting a minimum amount of retransmissions or using energetically conservative paths. The usage of broadcast communications for deploying information-centric mobile *ad hoc* networks (MANET) has been corroborated by the analytical results found by [VAR 11].

However the previously cited works address mobility from a static content perspective, letting dynamic and real-time content access as separate problems yet to be solved. Content provider relocation can lead to a series of events such as the impossibility of name aggregation due to the prefix dispersion over the network, the invalidation of pre-existing routes and obsolescence of already issued content requests, among others, which hinder the continuity of ongoing flows. Such factors may lead to discontinuities in these flows, causing severe reduction in the quality of the content delivery service to the end users. [KIM 12] shows that traditional solutions, like proxy servers and the use of indirection nodes, add significant delay to the content source relocation process. The study therefore proposes a forwarding mechanism that allows preservation of ongoing content flows during relocation of a data source, preserving the already published content names. Upon the data source handoff notification, content requests are stored for later forwarding. At the end of the physical relocation process, the data source sends a virtual content request to the previously served prefix. Thus, when forwarded by intermediate routers towards a data sources previous location, this virtual request allows nodes to update their forwarding tables with new routing metrics for that prefix, which will end up pointing to its new location. Upon reaching the last router of the old route, the virtual request starts the stored requests forwarding, which are delivered to the data source in its new location, completing the handoff process. After all existing data flows are completed, the data source can republish its content prefix in order to allow new requests to reach it.

4.6. Applications

Although ICN is a recent research domain, and consequently, with several open questions, there are many works focusing on new applications to the new paradigm of information-centric network. Some of these applications present already solid results. One of the first proposals addresses real-time applications, especially, VoIP.

4.6.1. *Real-time applications*

Although information-centric networks increase the efficiency of content distribution applications, it is necessary to investigate the performance of typical conversational applications such as electronic mail and voice transmission over IP networks (Voice over IP), since in ICN content is routed based on its name rather than on its IP address.

Jacobson *et al.* [JAC 09b] proposed and implemented a telephony application on the CCN architecture, named VoCCN. The main goal is to show the feasibility of mapping conversational protocols, such as Session Initiation Protocol (SIP) and Real-time Transfer Protocol (RTP), into content-based models. Therefore, the authors identify two main problems: how to start a call and how the receiver identifies and responds to the originator. On the current Internet, a port number is used as a meeting place for making calls. To initiate a call, the caller must request the establishment of a connection to the receiver, whose address is known, by sending packets with the specific port number. The receiver, in its turn, sends acknowledgment packets back to confirm a connection establishment, since the received packets have the address of the originator. In the CCN architecture, this is not trivial.

It is necessary to implement an on-demand publishing mechanism to initiate a call. As discussed in section 3.3, the

CCN architecture does not require that content must be published and registered in the infrastructure before any request. Accordingly, users might submit requests for contents that have not yet been published. These requests are forwarded to potential publishers that create and publish the content in response to the received request. Thus, the call is initiated. The second problem lies in enabling the publisher to send content back to the consumer, since packets do not bring any identification of the user who has requested the content. The solution is to use constructible names. The idea is to be able to build the name of a given chunk without prior knowledge of information about that content. To ensure this property, the publisher and the consumer must use a deterministic algorithm that allows them to build the same name and that enables consumers to request content with partially specified names [JAC 09b]. Once the constructible names property is assured, the publisher can receive a packet of interest and, consequently, create a content named according to the information contained in this packet, and send a data packet. This packet is then routed back to the consumer by the reverse path constructed from the crumbs left by the packet of interest. Hence, it creates a bidirectional flow of data between consumer and publisher.

Experimental results show that the application VoCCN is simpler, safer and more scalable than an equivalent VoIP application based on the current Internet architecture. It is worth noticing that VoCCN maintains interoperability with current applications, because it uses standard implementations of SIP and RTP protocols, and a simple and stateless IP-to-CCN gateway.

An application similar to VoCCN, named VoPSI, is proposed by Stais et al. [STA 11] for the PSIRP architecture, presented in section 3.4. Another application, Audio Conference Tool (ACT), is an extension of VoCCN that implements audio conferencing features, such as the discovery of ongoing conferences and its participants [ZHU 11]. Tsilopoulos and Xylomenos [TSI 11] propose mechanisms of traffic differentiation for ICNs. The idea is that the content is forwarded not only according to its name, but also to its type. Contents are categorized into two groups: documents and channels. Chunks sensitive to losses are classified as documents. Otherwise, they are classified as channels. Besides, the documents are divided into two groups: on-demand and real time. In general, multimedia applications are classified as channels. File transfer, video over HTTP and email are on-demand documents. Finally, online games, chat rooms and instant messengers are real-time documents.

4.6.2. *Vehicular networks*

Vehicular networks have received significant attention in the last few years [RUB 09], especially with the advent of the concept of DTNs [KHA 12, FAL 08]. These networks are characterized by an important intermittent connectivity, which might cause substantial message delivery delay and a poor delivery rate [FAL 03]. As a result, the traditional TCP/IP stack does not fit well because it assumes there is always an end-to-end path between source and destination. Therefore, the basic principle adopted in vehicular networks consists of store-carry and forward approach to overcome the performance problems already mentioned. In this approach, nodes aggregate messages in bundles and are equipped with buffers. Thus, nodes keep these bundles in the buffer during connectionless periods and try to forward them whenever a contact is established with a neighbor. As a consequence, the forwarding mechanism and the discarding policies play a significant role in the performance of vehicular networks. Hence, several works have addressed these issues [VAH 00, NAV 12, MIR 12, KHA 12]. However, due to the lack of mobility patterns in most of cases, delivering bundles is not a trivial task and is still a challenge. Recent works have investigated the feasibility of employing a content-centric approach to improve the efficiency of vehicular networks [AMA 12a, ARN 11, TAL 12]. Amadeo *et al.* propose a content-centric framework for vehicular networks, which is implemented on top of IEEE 802.11p standard [AMA 12b].

4.6.3. *Autonomous driving*

The concept of autonomous driving lies in building vehicles that control their own motion in highways and urban streets. Thus, autonomous vehicles are capable of sensing their environment and navigating without human assistance. Autonomous driving has received significant attention lately due to advances in sensing and computation technologies [CAM 10, URM 09]. The main challenges in developing autonomous driving are [URM 09]:

– systems integration – to integrate numerous technological solutions, such as sensors, hardware, software and algorithms;

– prediction and trust – to predict the behavior of other vehicles, anticipating their actions and consider this information at the planning phase. It is also important to incorporate into the prediction the notion of trust, which refers to the extent in which we can trust in other vehicles to respect traffic rules;

– interactions between agents – to support inter-vehicle communications to allow vehicles to share experiences and to exchange information about driving decisions;

– learning – to learn from previous experiences to be able to adapt to new situations;

– scaling up – to allow the car go faster in a more complex environment, which is directly related to the response time of the system. The response time comprises the sensing delay, processing data delay, decision-making delay, command to actuators delay, the actuator response delay and the car response delay;

– verification and validation – to verify that the systems operate safely and robustly.

It is clear that communication plays a significant role in autonomous vehicle systems. In this context, CarSpeak is a communication system that addresses all the main challenges of autonomous driving [KUM 12]. In the proposed system, vehicles are able to request and access sensory information from the static infrastructure, as well as from other vehicles. CarSpeak applies the concept of information-centric networks to improve the efficiency of the system. The basic idea consists of dividing the sensory data by regions, which is recursively divided into cubes. Hence, upon receiving a request for information about a specific region, all cars that have sensor data about this region can send all or some part (cubes) of the information. Interestingly enough, the author incorporates the paradigm of information-centric networks into a Medium Access Mechanism (MAC). In the content-centric MAC, the information objects contend for medium access, instead of the senders. Thus, the medium is shared proportionally to the popularity of the information object, namely the number of requests an information object receives.

4.6.4. Other applications

There are many other applications that can benefit from the ICN paradigm, such as for instance using a content-centric communication infrastructure for gaming applications [CHE 12], improving the network performance of healthcare services [UAR 12], improving P2P real-time group communication [LUK 12], and using ICN to offload cellular networks [DET 12b], saving the network load in social networks [MAT 12].

5

Practical Issues

Various architectures, such as those described in Chapter 3, are evaluated in test beds in which experimental prototypes of their protocol stacks are used, as is the case with CCNx[1]. To use these proposals on a large scale, it is necessary however to define practical implementation issues of ICNs. The two main issues are: the definition of an economic model for a new Internet based on ICNs and the deployment of content routers. In the following, these practical issues are discussed.

5.1. Economic models

For the adoption of ICNs on a large scale, it is essential to define a model that encourages current network operators and service providers to migrate to an ICN architecture and ensures remuneration for their activities, even with the adoption of new technologies [FEA 07].

The current business model adopted for the Internet is based on connectivity. In general, users pay their local ISPs for access to the network [TRO 10a]. The role of an ISP, in

---

1 http://www.ccnx.org.

this case, is simply forwarding packets. As the network services are provided end-to-end and the Internet is organized into autonomous systems, ISPs also pay to send their traffic to other ISPs.

The basic packet delivery services are becoming commodities and, thus, ISPs are looking for new services to increase their revenues [FEA 07]. Currently, there are services that offer differentiated distribution of voice and video to users who pay more for such differentiation [TRO 10a]. Another example in this direction are the CDNs that adopt a particular business model. A CDN provider offers its services to producers who pay to distribute their content to consumers more efficiently. The CDN provider has a central platform that coordinates the service provision, guarantees a specific service level and is responsible for charging users. However, this model is not efficient for ICNs, since it is based on a strong central element and, therefore, affects the scalability of such networks.

Although there is still no definition of economic models to be adopted in ICNs, some proposals do exist [TRO 10b, ZHA 11, BIR 11]. Zhang et al. define the actors of a business model for ICNs [ZHA 11]. The actors are the content producers, who create content, the content providers, which are the servers that aggregate content from different producers and consumers that request the content. The authors also consider the existence of datacenter providers, which offer storage and processing resources, and ISPs, which are divided into Internet Access Network Providers (IAPs) and Internet Backbone Providers (IBPs). Finally, there are advertisers, which correlate their brand with the content during the distribution process, and sponsors that add content to their brands during the production phase. These actors work within the two layers proposed for content distribution: the content production layer and the interconnection layer.

The content production layer is at the highest level, in which the data unit can consist of digital objects such as video, music and files. Figure 5.1a) shows a simplified value network[2] for the production layer which shows (1) the process of creating and publishing content, (2) the different storage possibilities of contents and (3) the different sources of revenue from the content provider. The nodes represent actors, and the arrows that interconnect nodes represent the traffic and monetary exchanges, as well as intangible benefits among the stakeholders.

The possibility of storing contents in all elements of the network provides a traffic reduction and, consequently, a routing cost reduction. However, it introduces new challenges related to pricing and the management of ICNs. Reducing the routing cost, for instance, is obtained in exchange for storage in the network. Currently, this exchange is interesting since the storage cost decays faster than the transmission cost. However, the comparison between the costs of both is difficult because storage and transmission are priced differently [BIR 11]. In general, the user pays for a given storage capacity that is dedicated and can be reused multiple times. The same content, for example, can be accessed multiple times in cache and the user is not charged by the number of hits, but by the storage space occupied by the content. On the other hand, forwarding is a pay-per-use type of service, namely, reforwarding implies invoicing for the same package.

---

2 A value network is a method used to analyze business models that describes technical and social resources, and illustrates the interconnections between the different actors in the model.

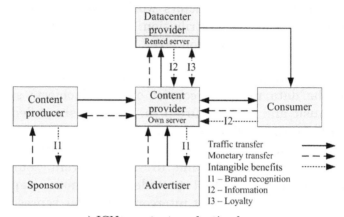

a) ICN – content production layer

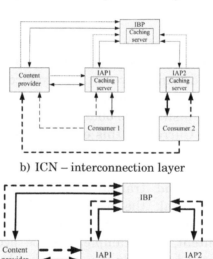

b) ICN – interconnection layer

c) Client–server – interconnection layer

Figure 5.1. *Value networks for ICNs and for the client–server model*

Another key issue is whether the cache should be transparent or based on commercial agreements. For most of the ICN architectures, caching is transparent, that is all routers store content regardless of who publishes it or requests it. However, nowadays in CDNs caching is based on trade agreements with great success [BIR 11]. Besides, there is still no definition of who should decide about storing a given content in a network element: the ISP and/or the content provider. In case both have control, conflicts may exist and, thus, it is necessary to develop multipartite control. For example, IAPs can update their cache with a frequency lower than the cache expected by the content provider. Contractual measures and monetary incentives can resolve this conflict. In this scenario, there may exist a content regulator that is responsible for resolving conflicts of interest between the network actors, which can be consumers, ISPs and content providers. The regulator can classify, for example, a certain content as private, meaning that it should not be stored by any network element, or it can determine which content each element is allowed to store. Another important issue that still remains an open question lies in deciding whether end systems will also participate in the caching system or just network elements such as routers and cache servers. The two solutions are currently implemented by the CDNs and P2P networks, respectively. Both are also considered by different ICN architectures [ZHU 10].

A key issue for adopting ICN on a large scale is to encourage ISPs to change the current business model. Nowadays, as suggested by the great success experienced by CDNs, content providers are more willing to pay for differentiated services than ISPs [TRO 10a]. However, ISPs have a fundamental role in adopting ICNs, since they are responsible to provide caches. The IAPs can be convinced by the possibility of interdomain traffic and costs reduction with the adoption of a universal cache. Currently, IBPs suffer from a decrease in the traffic exchange prices and, thus, they are looking for new sources of revenue [ZHA 11]. Several IBPs have also become CDN providers, which may suggest that they are open to the new changes introduced by the ICNs.

5.2. Content routers

The implementation of content routers is a major challenge for the development of ICNs [AHL 08, ARI 10b, PER 11, TRO 12]. These routers, unlike traditional ones, are not merely responsible for forwarding packets, route calculations and updating routing tables. In content routers, content storage becomes an internal operation of routers and not a coordinated procedure for other network elements [ARI 10b]. Therefore, each router is responsible for the cache management, which comprises storage and replacement policies. Besides, routers should be able to search content in its cache before forwarding a content request. In addition, routers must keep information about requests in order to forward it back to the users who have requested each content.

Currently, there are several proposals to introduce caches in traditional IP routers in order to remove redundant packets from the network [ANA 08, ANA 09]. These mechanisms, however, differ from content routers because they are based on the adoption of codecs and decoders in different network elements and requires coordination between these elements.

The introduction of operations related to content storage management requires hardware and software modifications on current routers. The name-based routing and the content cache at the granularity of packets requires higher processing capacity than those of current routers. The adoption of a local cache, in this case, can reduce the number of forward operations performed by a router. Another important requirement is to increase the amount of storage capacity of routers due to the expected increase in namespace. Currently, this space consists of one billion IP addresses; however, there will be at least a trillion content names [PER 11].

Arianfar *et al.* [ARI 10b] assess the feasibility of using content routers based on the settings of hardware and software current available in routers. For this purpose, the authors define a reference model for a content router and propose mechanisms to implement their features. The model considers the implementation of a CS, as defined in the CCN architecture, shown in Figure 3.2, and the memory hierarchy into three levels, adopted in current standard routers that use content-addressable memory (CAM), static random access memory (SRAM) and dynamic random access memory (DRAM). The CS consists of two main components: the memory cache and an indexing table. Each table entry contains the identifier of the packet, its memory address in the cache and packet status information. The indexing table entries are shared between the DRAM and SRAM to reduce the amount of SRAM memory used, and hence the cost of the equipment, as shown in Table 5.1. The cache uses only DRAM.

Type	Access time (ms)	Maximum size	Cost (USD/MB)	Energy consumption (W/MB)
TCAM	4	≈ 20 Mb	200	15
SRAM	0.45	≈ 210 Mb	27	0.12
RLDRAM	15	≈ 2 Gb	0.27	0.027
DRAM	55	≈ 10 GB	0.016	0.023
High-speed SSD	1.000	≈ 10 TB	0.03	0,00005
SSD	10.000	≈ 1 TB	0.003	0.00001

Table 5.1. *The main parameters for each memory type [PER 11]*

The features of a content router defined by Arianfar *et al.* are the insertion, removal and search element of content packets in the CS, as well as, the identification, queuing and forwarding of packets. Based on these definitions, we can estimate the computational resources required by each feature individually. The authors evaluate the processing power, the memory access time, the memory space required to store content and the energy consumption.

The processing power is not a critical factor. The operations related to the CS involves searching, verifying and updating the indexing table, which requires fewer clock cycles considering the use of Application-Specific Integrated Circuits (ASICs) and Field-Programmable Gate Arrays (FPGAs). Moreover, the memory access time can be a bottleneck. The access time of a DRAM is typically in the order of 50 ns and the intervals between the arrival of packets of 40 bytes in links of 10 Gb/s (OC-192) and 40 Gb/s (OC-768) are 32 and 8 ns, respectively. In this case, the simplest solution to avoid the bottleneck is to use memory banks in parallel or by replacing the current DRAMs by faster memories, such as reduced latency DRAMs (RLDRAMs), which have access times in the order of 15 ns, as shown in Table 5.1. To assess the memory space required to store the content, the authors assume that a router stores all traffic passing through a network interface of 10 Gb/s in a time interval of 10 s. Nowadays this requires a DRAM memory space approximately of 100 Gb, costing up to $300. Besides, the estimation for the *indexing table* is around nine million entries of 36 bits, which is stored in the SRAM. Thus, it takes 324 Mb with an approximate current cost of $500. Hence, the total memory cost per port for a router is $800. In 2011, a commercial 10 Gb/s router has an average cost per port ranging from $1,500 to 2,500. Therefore, the adaptation of a conventional router to a content router would increase by up to 30% the cost per port. The growth in energy consumption by each interface, due to the increase of memory space, would be in the order of 100 kWh/year, which implies an additional cost of $20 and represents a small portion of the total energy consumption of the equipment. Therefore, the authors conclude that the making conventional routers into content routers is feasible in terms of the additional resources required and the associated costs.

Perino and Varvello [PER 11] also analyze the feasibility of implementing content routers using current hardware and software settings. However, they use a more complex reference model for content routers, which takes into account the other components of a CCN router besides the CS. The model considers the FIB and the PIT. Basically, each component is modeled individually according to the arrival rate of interest and data packets, as well as the service rate of each element. From this model and considering different metrics, the authors evaluate router components individually – CS, FIB and PIT – and suggest that different types of memory should be used by each router. The CS performance is evaluated based on the hit rate of the content cache. Intuitively, the higher is the probability of finding a content in the CS that corresponds to a request, the lower is the amount of requests sent to the FIB. However, this procedure only occurs if the memory used to store the indexing table is fast enough to process all packets arriving at the CS. Otherwise, packets will be forwarded directly to the FIB. Thus, to ensure an accuracy rate of 90%, which is similar to a traditional CDN, SRAM and RLDRAM memories should be used to store the indexing table. The PIT is assessed in terms of the interest packet arrival rate, which in the worst case scenario, equals the arrival rate of requests at the CS. Therefore, the estimated size for the PIT is 1.4 Gb, considering one link input of 100 Gb/s and, thus, RLDRAM can be used. Finally, the search in the FIB is evaluated according to the number of content prefixes. To ensure a sole access to the external memory (off-chip) per search, in a

200 Mb memory space, the maximum number of prefixes is 20 million [PER 11]. This number of prefixes corresponds to 25% of the names of active hosts on the current Internet. On the basis of these results, the authors conclude that a content router adapted from current routers cannot operate at Internet scale, but that it works well at the scale of a CDN or an ISP.

Perino and Varvello also presented two possible configurations for content core routers and content edge routers. The amount of additional memory to convert each router is determined according to the arrival rate of packets of interest per second. The goal of the analysis is to estimate the additional cost and power consumption of the equipment. The model used as a border router is a Cisco 7507 that has 5 Gb Ethernet network interfaces. To make it into a content router that supports a rate of 15 Mpck/s, the following equipment should be used: (1) a high-speed Solid-State Drive (SSD) memory of 1 TB to implement the CS, (2) a 6 GB DRAM for the indexing table, (3) a 70 Mb RLDRAM for the PIT, (4) a 200 Mb SRAM for the internal memory of the FIB and (5) a 140 MB DRAM for the external memory of the FIB. These additional features would increase by 195 W the peak energy consumption and by approximately $30,000 the price of the equipment. The core router model used in the analysis is a Cisco CRS 1 with eight network interfaces of 40 Gb/s. To transform it into a content router that allows an arrival rate of 1 Gpck/s and to store 250 million prefixes, a CS per interface is necessary, each with 10 GB of DRAM and an indexing table of 266 Mb duplicated on two RLDRAM chips, a PIT per interface with 560 Mb SRAM, 4 Gb SRAM to implement the internal memory of the FIB and 1.5 GB DRAM for the FIB external memory. These additional features would increase by approximately 3,000 W the consumption peak and by $130,000 the price of the equipment. Recently, Varvello et al. [VAR 12] introduced

Caesar, a content router prototype that performs name-based routing at high speed.

Wählisch *et al.* [WÄH 12] aim at evaluating in practice the performance of CCN routers for different loads. For this, they considered a different number of parallel downloads of 10 Mb files: two, 10 and 100 files. The experimental scenario is very simple: two CCNx routers interconnected at 100 Mb/s and one content consumer and one content repository connected to each one. The download time of files and the resource consumption on routers, that is the size of PIT, are observed. Results show that an increasing number of parallel downloads increases significantly the download time. In the worst case scenario, each file is received after 150 s while the link capacity allows us to retrieve all files in approximately 10 s. To explain this, the authors argue that the higher the download frequency, the higher is the number of simultaneous PIT entries. In addition, one file is composed of several chunks that are requested individually. Consequently, routers must maintain more states, which leads to a higher consumption of memory and the central processing unit (CPU). Only after receiving the data required by an interest packet, is the memory released. The authors claim that the exhaustion of resources is not due to the shortcomings of the CCNx implementation, but it is driven by the concept. One possible solution is to limit the transmission rate of interest packets per user.

Ul Haque *et al.* [ULH 12] analyze different blind routing algorithms[3] to deal with FIB's misses that may occur in CCN routers. The problem is that the namespace increases, as detailed before, because names are considered instead of addresses to undertake route decisions. Thus, CCN routers

---

3 Algorithms considered when the location of the requested data is not known.

should store a large set of entries in FIB but, currently, they are not able to do this. In this case, if an interest packet reaches a router and no route is found to the content desired, it is discarded. This is referred to as a FIB miss. An alternative to reduce the impact of misses is to search nearby routers to find a route for the desired content. Therefore, the authors implemented three blind routing algorithms over CCNx: flooding, expanding ring and random walk, and carried out simulations to evaluate them. Finally, they concluded that the random walk algorithm with queries sent on half of the total links provides the best performance in terms of end-to-end delay and routing overhead.

Li *et al.* [LI 12] also investigated scalability of naming mechanisms, in particular, the CCN hierarchical naming mechanism. The authors introduced a framework of fast longest-prefix name lookup and presented an experimental evaluation of this approach. The key idea is to produce compressed unstructured keys and store these keys in FIB rather than hierarchical names. The advantage is that the key space is much smaller than the name prefix space and keys are easier to manipulate than prefixes. In this approach, CCN routers must have two paths: a slow path that deals with name prefix announcements and a fast path used to forward interest packets. When a CCN router receives a name prefix announcement, it forwards it to the slow path that transforms the hierarchically structured name prefix into a compressed key. This procedure is called a reduction algorithm. After that, the update algorithm adds into FIB the transformed key. To reduce the collision probability, authors use a dual-hash approach to generate keys [LI 12]. In the fast path, a CCN router first applies the key set generation algorithm to the name extracted from the interest packet received. The result is a set of unstructured keys that will be used during the longest-prefix name lookup. In this case, the reduction algorithm cannot be directly applied to the name in order to produce a key and to use it for lookup. The reduction algorithm loses the hierarchical structure carried by CCN names. Without hierarchy, it is not possible to look up in the reduced key space the longest name prefix that matches the name. The solution to maintain the hierarchical structure of the CCN name is to iteratively apply the name reduction algorithm to the different segments of the name. Let us assume that segments are separated by the slash/(– and the algorithm starts from the leftmost n segments to produce K_n. For example, for the name /uff.br/videos/class1, the iterative reduction algorithm will produce three keys: K_1 for /uff.br/, K_2 for /uff.br/videos/ and K_3 for /uff.br/videos/class1. Thus, a CCN router is able to perform the longest name prefix by looking for a route entry related to these keys. The authors experimentally evaluated the proposed framework on a PC equipped with an Intel® Xeon® X5675 processor with 24 GB main memory. They used a data set collected from tier-1 ISP networks with 6.0 million uniform resource locators (URLs). The main conclusion was that the proposed framework achieves a name lookup throughput up to 37 M packet lookups per second.

Conclusion

The traffic generated by content distribution applications corresponds to more than a half of the current Internet traffic [SAN 11]. In Brazil, for example, 53% of traffic comes from P2P file-sharing systems and multimedia streaming applications. In North America and Europe, this percentage achieves 60% [SAN 11]. Although content distribution applications already have millions of users and, in particular cases, experience a great commercial success, the current Internet architecture imposes technical barriers that significantly increases the complexity to implement and manage such applications. In practice, current applications are still mostly working because of the "patches" applied to the Internet. These patches may compromise network scalability and are proprietary solutions, in most cases. In addition, solutions such as P2P systems and content distribution networks run as overlays and do not take into account the underlying network topology to increase the content distribution efficiency.

ICNs, in this context, are an alternative and promising network substrate not only to develop content distribution but also for conversational applications. The main advantage of the ICN paradigm is to intrinsically provide efficient resource and data sharing, mechanisms to increase content availability, intrinsic content security and mobility support. ICN-based solutions, in general, are simpler than the proposals for the current Internet.

Ongoing studies are mainly focused on new architectures for ICNs and also on the evaluation of cache policies. However, the development of ICNs faces non-technical challenges related to the actors involved in the content distribution. There are conflicts of interest in the peering between providers and no incentives to adopt cache in access networks and it is hard to provide content-access accounting. ICN standardization and interoperability between different ICN architectures are also open problems. Currently, there are Internet Engineering Task Force (IETF) groups working on the standardization of in-network packet storage (DECADE) [SON 12] and also on interconnection between CDNs (CDNI) [NIV 12]. Unfortunately, there are no initiatives to define mechanisms to provide interoperability between ICN architectures, such as CCN and DONA.

Undoubtedly, the roadmap to ICN development includes several technical and economic challenges that demand huge research effort. The results of these actions, however, will radically change the current Internet communication paradigm.

Acknowledgment

This work is supported by CNPq, CAPES, FAPERJ, FINEP, CTIC and FUNTTEL.

Bibliography

[AHL 08] AHLGREN B., D'AMBROSIO M., MARCHISIO M., *et al.*, "Design considerations for a network of information", *Re-Architecting the Internet Workshop – ReARCH*, pp. 66:1–66:6, December 2008.

[AKA 12] AKAMAI TECHNOLOGIES, "Akamai handles a significant portion of World Wide Web traffic – over a trillion interactions every day", http://www.akamai.com/html/about/index.html, 2012, Accessed 12 March 2012.

[AMA 12a] AMADEO M., CAMPOLO C., MOLINARO A., "Content-centric networking: is that a solution for upcoming vehicular networks?", *ACM International Workshop on Vehicular Internetworking, Systems, and Applications, VANET*, June 2012.

[AMA 12b] AMADEO M., CAMPOLO C., MOLINARO A., "CRoWN: content-centric networking in vehicular ad hoc networks", *IEEE Communications Letters*, vol. 16, no. 9, pp. 1380–1383, September 2012.

[ANA 08] ANAND A., GUPTA A., AKELLA A., *et al.*, "Packet caches on routers: the implications of universal redundant traffic elimination", *ACM Special Interest Group on Data Communication Conference – SIGCOMM*, pp. 219–230, August 2008.

[ANA 09] ANAND A., SEKAR V., AKELLA A., "SmartRE: an architecture for coordinated network-wide redundancy elimination", *ACM Special Interest Group on Data Communication Conference – SIGCOMM*, pp. 87–98, August 2009.

[ARI 10a] ARIANFAR S., NIKANDER P., OTT J., Packet-level Caching for Information-centric Networking, Report, Aalto University, June 2010.

[ARI 10b] ARIANFAR S., NIKANDER P., OTT J., "On content-centric router design and implications", *Re-Architecting the Internet Workshop – ReARCH*, pp. 5:1–5:6, November 2010.

[ARI 11] ARIANFAR S., KOPONEN T., RAGHAVAN B. *et al.*, "On preserving privacy in content-oriented networks", *ACM SIGCOMM Workshop on Information-Centric Networking – ICN*, pp. 19–24, August 2011.

[ARN 11] ARNOULD G., KHADRAOUI D., HABBAS Z., "A self-organizing content centric network model for hybrid vehicular ad-hoc networks", *ACM International Symposium on Design and Analysis of Intelligent Vehicular Networks and Applications, DIVANet '11*, October 2011.

[BAL 07] BALDONI R., BERALDI R., QUEMA V., *et al.*, "TERA: topic-based event routing for peer-to-peer architectures", *ACM International Conference on Distributed Event-Based Systems – DEBS*, pp. 2–13, June 2007.

[BAR 12] BARI M.F., CHOWDHURY S.R., AHMED R., *et al.*, "A survey of naming and routing in information-centric networks", *IEEE Communications Magazine*, vol. 50, no. 12, pp. 44–53, 2012.

[BAU 12] BAUGHER M., DAVIE B., NARAYANAN A. *et al.*, "Self-verifying names for read-only named data", *Workshop on Emerging Design Choices in Name-Oriented Networking – NOMEN*, pp. 274–279, March 2012.

[BHA 03] BHATTACHARYYA S., An overview of source-specific multicast (SSM), IETF Network Working Group RFC 3569, July 2003.

[BIR 11] BIRAGHI A.M., GONÁLVES J., LEVÄ T., *et al.*, New business models and business dynamics of the future networks, Report no. FP7-ICT-2009-5-257448-SAIL/D.A.7, Scalable and Adaptable Internet Solutions (SAIL) Project, July 2011.

[BRE 99] BRESLAU L., CAO P., FAN L., *et al.*, "Web caching and Zipf-like distributions: evidence and implications", *IEEE Conference on Computer Communications – INFOCOM*, pp. 126–134, March 1999.

[BRO 03] BRODER A., MITZENMACHER M., "Network applications of bloom filters: a survey", *Internet Mathematics*, vol. 1, no. 4, pp. 485–509, 2003.

[BUY 08] BUYYA R., PATHAN M., VAKALI A., *Content Delivery Networks*, Springer, 1st edition, 2008.

[CAE 06] CAESAR M., CONDIE T., KANNAN J., *et al.*, "ROFL: routing on flat labels", *ACM Special Interest Group on Data Communication Conference – SIGCOMM*, pp. 363–374, August 2006.

[CAM 10] CAMPBELL M., EGERSTEDT M., HOW J.P. *et al.*, "Autonomous driving in urban environments: approaches, lessons and challenges", *Philosophical Transactions of the Royal Society*, vol. 368, no. 1928, pp. 4649–4672, October 2010.

[CAO 04] CAO F., SINGH J.P., "Efficient event routing in content-based publish-subscribe service networks", *IEEE Conference on Computer Communications – INFOCOM*, March 2004.

[CAR 00] CARZANIGA A., ROSENBLUM D.S., WOLF A.L., Content-based addressing and routing: a general model and its application, Report no. CU-CS-902-00, Department of Computer Science, University of Colorado, January 2000.

[CAR 01] CARZANIGA A., ROSENBLUM D.S., WOLF A.L., "Design and evaluation of a wide-area event notification service", *ACM Transactions on Computer Systems*, vol. 19, no. 3, pp. 332–383, August 2001.

[CAR 03] CARZANIGA A., WOLF A.L., "Forwarding in a content-based network", *ACM Special Interest Group on Data Communication Conference – SIGCOMM*, pp. 163–174, August 2003.

[CAR 04] CARZANIGA A., RUTHERFORD M.J., WOLF A.L., "A Routing scheme for content-based networking", *IEEE Conference on Computer Communications – INFOCOM*, pp. 918–928, March 2004.

[CAR 09] CARZANIGA A., CARUGHI G.T., HALL C. *et al.*, Practical high-throughput content-based routing using unicast state and probabilistic encodings, Report no. 2009/06, Faculty of Informatics, University of Lugano, August 2009.

[CAR 11a] CAROFIGLIO G., GALLO M., MUSCARIELLO L., "Bandwidth and storage sharing performance in information centric networking", *ACM SIGCOMM Workshop on Information-Centric Networking – ICN*, pp. 26–31, August 2011.

[CAR 11b] CAROFIGLIO G., GALLO M., MUSCARIELLO L., *et al.*, "Modeling data transfer in content-centric networking", *International Teletraffic Congress – ITC*, pp. 111–118, August 2011.

[CAR 11c] CAROFIGLIO G., GEHLEN V., PERINO D., "Experimental evaluation of memory management in content-centric networking", *IEEE International Communications Conference – ICC*, pp. 1–6, June 2011.

[CHA 12] CHAI W.K., HE D., PSARAS I., *et al.*, "Collaborative forwarding and caching in content centric networks", *IFIP International Conferences on Networking – Networking*, May 2012.

[CHE 00] CHERITON D., GRITTER M., TRIAD: A new next generation Internet architecture, Report, Computer Science Department, Stanford University, 2000.

[CHE 01] CHE H., WANG Z., TUNG Y., "Analysis and design of hierarchical Web caching systems", *IEEE Conference on Computer Communications – INFOCOM*, pp. 1416–1424, April 2001.

[CHE 02] CHE H., TUNG Y., WANG Z., "Hierarchical Web caching systems: modeling, design and experimental results", *IEEE Journal on Selected Areas in Communications*, vol. 20, no. 7, pp. 1305–1314, September 2002.

[CHE 12] CHEN J., ARUMAITHURAI M., FU X., *et al.*, "G-COPSS: a content centric communication infrastructure for gaming applications", *IEEE International Conference on Distributed Computing Systems, ICDCS'12*, June 2012.

[CHO 07] CHOCKLER G., MELAMED R., TOCK Y., *et al.*, "SpiderCast: a scalable interest-aware overlay for topic-based pub/sub communication", *ACM International Conference on Distributed Event-Based Systems – DEBS*, pp. 14–25, June 2007.

[CHO 09] CHOI J., HAN J., CHO E., *et al.*, "Performance comparison of content-oriented networking alternatives: a hierarchical tree versus a flat distributed hash table", *IEEE Conference on Local Computer Networks – LCN*, pp. 253–256, October 2009.

[CHO 11] CHOI J., HAN J., CHO E., *et al.*, "A survey on content-oriented networking for efficient content delivery", *IEEE Communications Magazine*, vol. 49, no. 3, pp. 121–127, March 2011.

[CHO 12] CHO K., LEE M., PARK K., *et al.*, "WAVE: popularity-based and collaborative in-network caching for content-oriented networks", *Workshop on Emerging Design Choices in Name-Oriented Networking – NOMEN*, March 2012.

[CLA 01] CLARKE D.E., ELIEN J.-E., ELLISON C.M., *et al.*, "Certificate chain discovery in SPKI/SDSI", *Journal of Computer Security*, vol. 9, no. 4, pp. 285–322, 2001.

[COS 06] COSTA L.H.M.K., FDIDA S., DUARTE O.C.M.B., "Incremental service deployment using the hop by hop multicast routing protocol", *IEEE/ACM Transactions on Networking*, vol. 14, no. 3, pp. 543–556, June 2006.

[D'AM 11] D'AMBROSIO M., DANNEWITZ C., KARL H., *et al.*, "MDHT: a hierarquical name resolution service for information-centric networks", *ACM SIGCOMM Workshop on Information-Centric Networking – ICN*, August 2011.

[DAI 12] DAI J., HU Z., LI B., *et al.*, "Collaborative hierarchical caching with dynamic request routing for massive content distribution", *IEEE Conference on Computer Communications – INFOCOM*, March 2012.

[DAN 10] DANNEWITZ C., GOLIC J., OHLMAN B., *et al.*, "Secure naming for a network of information", *IEEE Global Internet Symposium – GI Symposium*, pp. 1–6, March 2010.

[DEE 89] DEERING S., Host extensions for IP multicasting, IETF Network Working Group RFC 1112, August 1989.

[DET 11] DETTI A., BLEFARI MELAZZI N., SALSANO S., *et al.*, "CONET: a content centric inter-networking architecture", *ACM SIGCOMM Workshop on Information-Centric Networking – ICN*, August 2011.

[DET 12a] DETTI A., SALSANO S., BLEFARI-MELAZZI N., IPv4 and IPv6 options to support information centric networking – draft-detti-conet-ip-option-04, IETF Network Working Informational Internet-Draft, November 2012.

[DET 12b] DETTI A., POMPOSINI M., BLEFARI-MELAZZI N., *et al.*, "Information-centric networking: a natural design for social network applications", *IEEE International Conference on a World of Wireless, Mobile and Multimedia Networks – WoWMoM'12*, June 2012.

[DIA 11] DIALLO M., FDIDA S., SOURLAS V., *et al.*, "Leveraging caching for Internet-scale content-based publish/subscribe networks", *IEEE International Communications Conference – ICC*, pp. 1–5, June 2011.

[DIB 11] DIBENEDETTO S., PAPADOPOULOS C., MASSEY D., "Routing policies in named data networking", *ACM SIGCOMM Workshop on Information-Centric Networking – ICN*, pp. 38–43, August 2011.

[EUG 03] EUGSTER P., FELBER P., GUERRAOUI R., *et al.*, "The many faces of publish/subscribe", *ACM Computing Surveys*, vol. 35, no. 2, pp. 114–131, June 2003.

[EUM 12] EUM S., NAKAUCHI K., MURATA M., *et al.*, "CATT: potential based routing with content caching for ICN", *ACM SIGCOMM Workshop on Information-Centric Networking – ICN*, pp. 49–54, August 2012.

[FAL 03] FALL K., "A delay-tolerant network architecture for challenged internets", *ACM Special Interest Group on Data Communication Conference – SIGCOMM*, August 2003.

[FAL 08] FALL K., FARRELL S., "DTN: an architectural retrospective", *IEEE Journal on Selected Areas of Communications (JSAC)*, vol. 26, no. 5, pp. 828–836, May 2008.

[FEA 07] FEAMSTER N., GAO L., REXFORD J., "How to lease the Internet in your spare time", *ACM SIGCOMM Computer Communication Review*, vol. 37, no. 1, pp. 61–64, January 2007.

[FOF 12] FOFACK N.C., NAIN P., NEGLIA G., *et al.*, "Analysis of TTL-based cache networks", *International Conference on Performance Evaluation Methodologies and Tools (VALUETOOLS'12)*, October 2012.

[FOT 10] FOTIOU N., NIKANDER P., TROSSEN D., *et al.*, "Developing information networking further: From PSIRP to PURSUIT", *ICST International Conference on Broadband Communications, Networks, and Systems – BROADNETS*, October 2010.

[FRI 12] FRICKER C., ROBERT P., ROBERTS J., *et al.*, "Impact of traffic mix on caching performance in a content-centric network", *Workshop on Emerging Design Choices in Name-Oriented Networking – NOMEN*, March 2012.

[GAN 04] GANESAN P., GUMMADI K., GARCIA-MOLINA H., "Canon in G major: designing DHTs with hierarchical structure", *International Conference on Distributed Computing Systems – ICDCS*, pp. 263–272, March 2004.

[GAO 06] GAO Y., DENG L., KUZMANOVIC A., *et al.*, "Internet cache pollution attacks and countermeasures", *IEEE International Conference on Network Protocols – ICNP*, pp. 54–64, November 2006.

[GHO 11a] GHODSI A., KOPONEN T., RAGHAVAN B., *et al.*, "Information-centric networking: seeing the forest for the trees", *ACM Workshop on Hot Topics in Networks – HotNets*, pp. 1:1–1:6, November 2011.

[GHO 11b] GHODSI A., KOPONEN T., RAJAHALME J., *et al.*, "Naming in content-oriented architectures", *ACM SIGCOMM Workshop on Information-Centric Networking – ICN*, pp. 1–6, August 2011.

[GUO 12] GUO S., XIE H., SHI G., "Cache "less for more" in information-centric networks", *IFIP International Conferences on Networking – Networking*, May 2012.

[HEI 06] HEISSENBUTTEL M., BRAUN T., WALCHLI M., *et al.*, "Optimized stateless broadcasting in wireless multi-hop networks", *IEEE Conference on Computer Communications – INFOCOM*, April 2006.

[HOL 06] HOLBROOK H., CAIN B., Source-specific multicast for IP, IETF Network Working Group RFC 4607, 2006.

[INT 03] INTANAGONWIWAT C., GOVINDAN R., ESTRIN D., *et al.*, "Directed diffusion for wireless sensor networking", *IEEE/ACM Transactions on Networking*, vol. 11, pp. 2–16, 2003.

[JAC 09a] JACOBSON V., SMETTERS D., THORNTON J., *et al.*, "Networking named content", *International Conference on emerging Networking EXperiments and Technologies – CoNEXT*, December 2009.

[JAC 09b] JACOBSON V., SMETTERS D.K., BRIGGS N.H., *et al.*, "VoCCN: voice-over content-centric networks", *Re-Architecting the Internet Workshop – ReARCH*, pp. 1–6, December 2009.

[JAC 12] JACOBSON V., SMETTERS D.K., THORNTON J.D., *et al.*, "Networking named content", *Communications of the ACM*, vol. 55, no. 1, pp. 117–124, January 2012.

[JOH 04] JOHNSON D., PERKINS C., ARKKO J., Mobility support in IPv6, IETF Network Working Group RFC 3775, June 2004.

[JOK 09] JOKELA P., ZAHEMSZKY A., ARIANFAR S., *et al.*, "LIPSIN: line speed publish/subscribe inter-networking", *ACM Special Interest Group on Data Communication Conference – SIGCOMM*, pp. 195–206, 2009.

[KAT 11] KATSAROS K.V., XYLOMENOS G., POLYZOS G.C., "MultiCache: an overlay architecture for information-centric networking", *Computer Networks*, vol. 55, no. 4, pp. 936–947, 2011.

[KHA 12] KHABBAZ M.J., ASSI C.M., FAWAZ W.F., "Disruption-tolerant networking: a comprehensive survey on recent developments and persisting challenges", *IEEE Communications Surveys & Tutorials*, vol. 14, no. 2, pp. 607–640, 2012.

[KIM 12] KIM D.-H., KIM J.-H., KIM Y.-S., *et al.*, "Mobility support in content centric networks", *ACM SIGCOMM Workshop on Information-Centric Networking – ICN*, August 2012.

[KOP 07] KOPONEN T., SHENKER S., STOICA I., *et al.*, "A data-oriented (and beyond) network architecture", *ACM Special Interest Group on Data Communication Conference – SIGCOMM*, pp. 181–192, August 2007.

[KUM 12] KUMAR S., SHI L., GIL S., *et al.*, "CarSpeak: a content-centric network for autonomous driving", *ACM Special Interest Group on Data Communication Conference – SIGCOMM*, August 2012.

[KUR 12] KUROSE J., "Content-centric networking: technical perspective", *Communications of the ACM*, vol. 55, no. 1, pp. 116–116, January 2012.

[LAG 10] LAGUTIN D., VISALA K., TARKOMA S., "Publish/subscribe for internet: PSIRP perspective", *Towards the Future Internet – Emerging Trends from European Research*, Chapter 8, pp. 75–84, IOS Press, 2010.

[LAO 06] LAOUTARIS N., CHE H., STAVRAKAKIS I., "The LCD interconnection of LRU caches and its analysis", *Performance Evaluation*, vol. 63, no. 7, pp. 609-634, July 2006.

[LAU 11] LAUFER R.P., VELLOSO P.B., DUARTE O.C.M.B., "Securing distributed network applications with generalized bloom filters", *Computer Networks*, vol. 55, no. 8, pp. 1804–1819, June 2011.

[LAU 12a] LAUFER R., DUBOIS-FERRIÈRE H., KLEINROCK L., "Polynomial-time algorithms for multirate anypath routing in wireless multihop networks", *IEEE Transactions on Networking*, vol. 20, no. 3, pp. 743–755, June 2012.

[LAU 12b] LAUFER R., VELLOSO P.B., VIEIRA L.F.M., *et al.*, "PLASMA: a new routing paradigm for wireless multihop networks", *IEEE Conference on Computer Communications – INFOCOM*, March 2012.

[LAU 12c] LAUINGER T., LAOUTARIS N., RODRIGUEZ P., *et al.*, "Privacy risks in named data networking: what is the cost of performance?", *ACM SIGCOMM Computer Communication Review*, vol. 45, no. 5, pp. 54–57, October 2012.

[LEE 11] LEE M., CHO K., PARK K., *et al.*, "SCAN: Scalable content routing for content-aware networking", *IEEE International Communications Conference – ICC*, pp. 1–5, June 2011.

[LI 11] LI B., LIU F., LI B., *et al.*, "Collaborative caching for video streaming among selfish wireless service providers", *IEEE Global Communication Conference – GLOBECOM*, December 2011.

[LI 12] LI F., CHEN F., WU J., *et al.*, "Fast longest prefix name lookup for content-centric network forwarding", *ACM/IEEE Symposium on Architectures for Networking and Communications Systems – ANCS*, pp. 73–74, October 2012.

[LIU 12] LIU H., DE FOY X., ZHANG D., "A multi-level DHT routing framework with aggregation", *ACM SIGCOMM Workshop on Information-Centric Networking – ICN*, pp. 43–48, August 2012.

[LU 04] LU Y., ABDELZAHER T.F., SAXENA A., "Design, implementation, and evaluation of differentiated caching services", *IEEE Transactions on Parallel and Distributed Systems*, vol. 15, no. 5, pp. 440–452, May 2004.

[LUK 12] LUK V. W.-H., WONG A. K.-S., LEA C.-T., *et al.*, "Peer-to-peer real-time group communication over content-centric network", *IEEE International Conference on High Performance Switching and Routing – HPSR'12*, June 2012.

[MAJ 09] MAJUMDER A., SHRIVASTAVA N., RASTOGI R. *et al.*, "Scalable content-based routing in pub/sub systems", *IEEE Conference on Computer Communications – INFOCOM*, pp. 567–575, April 2009.

[MAR 10] MARTINS J.L., DUARTE S., "Routing algorithms for content-based publish/subscribe systems", *IEEE Communications Surveys and Tutorials*, vol. 12, no. 1, pp. 39–58, 2010.

[MAT 12] MATHIEU B., TRUONG P., YOU W., *et al.*, "Measuring the capacity of in-car to in-car vehicular networks", *IEEE Communications Magazine*, vol. 5, no. 7, pp. 44–51, July 2012.

[MEA 02] MEALLING M., DENENBERG R.,   Report from the joint W3C/IETF URI planning interest group: uniform resource identifiers (URIs), URLs, and uniform resource names (URNs): clarifications and recommendations,   IETF Network Working Group RFC 3305, August 2002.

[MEI 10] MEISEL M., PAPPAS V., ZHANG L., "Ad hoc networking via named data", *ACM International Workshop on Mobility in the Evolving Internet Architecture – MobiArch*, September 2010.

[MIR 12] MIRANDA E.S., NAVES J.F., MORAES I.M., *et al.*, "A joint custody-based forwarding policy for delay-tolerant networks", *Global Information Infrastructure and Networking Symposium – GIIS'12*, December 2012.

[MOR 08] MORAES I.M., CAMPISTA M.E.M., DUARTE J.L., *et al.*, "On the impact of user mobility on peer-to-peer video streaming", *IEEE Wireless Communications Magazine*, vol. 15, no. 6, pp. 54–62, 2008.

[MOR 12] MOREIRA M.D.D., LAUFER R.P., VELLOSO P.B., *et al.*, "Capacity and robustness tradeoffs in Bloom filters for distributed applications", *IEEE Transactions on Parallel and Distributed Systems*, vol. 23, no. 12, pp. 2219–2230, December 2012.

[MOS 08] MOSKOWITZ R., NIKANDER P., JOKELA P., *et al.*, Host identity protocol, IETF Network Working Group RFC 5201, April 2008.

[NAU 06] NAUMOV V., BAUMANN R., GROSS T., "An evaluation of inter-vehicle ad hoc networks based on realistic vehicular traces", *ACM International Symposium on Mobile Ad Hoc Networking and Computing – MobiHoc*, May 2006.

[NAV 12] NAVES J.F., MORAES I.M., DE ALBUQUERQUE C. V.N., "LPS and LRF: efficient buffer management policies for delay and disruption tolerant networks", *IEEE Conference on Local Computer Networks – LCN*, October 2012.

[NI 99] NI S.-Y., TSENG Y.-C., CHEN Y.-S., *et al.*, "The broadcast storm problem in a mobile ad hoc network", *ACM International Conference on Mobile Computing and Networking – MobiCom*, August 1999.

[NIV 12] NIVEN-JENKINS B., FAUCHEUR F.L., BITAR N., Content distribution network interconnection (CDNI) problem statement, IETF Network Working Group Internet-Draft, March 2012.

[PAC 13] PACIFICI V., DAN G., "Content-peering dynamics of autonomous caches in a content-centric network", *IEEE Conference on Computer Communications – INFOCOM*, accepted for publication, March 2013.

[PAS 12] PASSARELLA A., "A survey on content-centric technologies for the current Internet: CDN and P2P solutions.", *Computer Communications*, vol. 35, no. 1, pp. 1–32, 2012.

[PER 11] PERINO D., VARVELLO M., "A reality check for content centric networking", *ACM SIGCOMM Workshop on Information-Centric Networking – ICN*, pp. 44–49, August 2011.

[PEY 98] PEYRAVIAN M., ROGINSKY A., KSHEMKALYANI A.D., "On probabilities of hash value matches", *Computers and Security*, vol. 17, no. 2, pp. 171-176, 1998.

[PLA 05] PLAGEMANN T., GOEBEL V., MAUTHE A., *et al.*, "From content distribution networks to content networks – issues and challenges", *International Journal for the Computer and Telecommunications Industry*, vol. 29, pp. 551–566, March 2005.

[POD 03] PODLIPNIG S., BSZRMENYI L., "A survey of Web cache replacement strategies", *ACM Computing Surveys*, vol. 35, no. 4, pp. 374–398, December 2003.

[POP 10] POPA L., GHODSI A., STOICA I., "HTTP as the narrow waist of the future internet", *ACM Workshop on Hot Topics in Networks – HotNets*, pp. 6:1–6:6, October 2010.

[POP 05] POPESCU B.C., VAN STEEN M., CRISPO B., *et al.*, "Securely replicated Web documents", *IEEE International Parallel and Distributed Processing Symposium – IPDPS*, pp. 104b–104b, April 2005.

[PSA 11] PSARAS I., CLEGG R.G., LANDA R., *et al.*, "Modelling and evaluation of CCN-caching trees", *IFIP International Conferences on Networking – Networking*, May 2011.

[PSA 12] PSARAS I., CHAI W.K., PAVLOU G., "Probabilistic in-network caching for information-centric networks", *ACM SIGCOMM Workshop on Information-Centric Networking – ICN*, pp. 55–60, August 2012.

[RAT 01] RATNASAMY S., FRANCIS P., HANDLEY M., *et al.*, "A scalable content-addressable network", *ACM Special Interest Group on Data Communication Conference – SIGCOMM*, pp. 161–172, August 2001.

[RAT 02] RATNASAMY S., STOICA I., SHENKER S., "Routing algorithms for DHTs: some open questions", *International Workshop on Peer-to-Peer Systems – IPTPS*, pp. 45–52, March 2002.

[ROS 09] ROSENSWEIG E.J., KUROSE J., "Breadcrumbs: efficient, best-effort content location in cache networks", *IEEE Conference on Computer Communications – INFOCOM*, pp. 2631–2635, April 2009.

[ROS 10] ROSENSWEIG E.J., KUROSE J., TOWSLEY D., "Approximate models for general cache networks", *IEEE Conference on Computer Communications – INFOCOM*, pp. 1–9, March 2010.

[ROS 11a] ROSSI D., ROSSINI G., Caching performance of content centric networks under multi-path routing (and more), Report, Telecom ParisTech, 2011.

[ROS 11b] ROSSI D., ROSSINI G., A dive into the caching performance of content centric networking, Report, Telecom ParisTech, 2011.

[ROS 12] ROSSI D., ROSSINI G., "On sizing CCN content store by exploiting topological information", *Workshop on Emerging Design Choices in Name-Oriented Networking – NOMEN*, March 2012.

[ROW 01] ROWSTRON A., DRUSCHEL P., "Pastry: scalable, decentralized object location, and routing for large-scale peer-to-peer systems", *ACM/IFIP/USENIX International Middleware Conference – Middleware*, pp. 329–350, November 2001.

[RUB 09] RUBINSTEIN M.G., ABDESSLEM F.B., CAVALCANTI S.R., et al., "Measuring the capacity of in-car to in-car vehicular networks", *IEEE Communications Magazine*, vol. 47, no. 11, pp. 128–136, November 2009.

[SAN 11] SANDVINE, Global Internet phenomena report, Report, Sandvine, October 2011.

[SAR 12] SAROLAHTI P., JUSSI KANGASHARJU J.O., "Locations vs. identities in internet content: applying information-centric principles in today's networks", *IEEE Communications Magazine*, vol. 50, no. 12, pp. 54–59, 2012.

[SME 09] SMETTERS D., JACOBSON V., Securing network content, Report no. TR-2009-1, Xerox Palo Alto Research Center – PARC, 2009.

[SOL 12] SOLLINS K.R., "Pervasive persistent identification for information centric networking", *ACM SIGCOMM Workshop on Information-Centric Networking – ICN*, pp. 1–6, August 2012.

[SON 12] SONG H., ZONG N., YANG Y., et al., "Decoupled application data enroute (DECADE) problem statement", IETF Network Working Group Internet-Draft, February 2012.

[SOU 11] SOURLAS V., FLEGKAS P., PASCHOS G.S., et al., "Storage planning and replica assignment in content-centric publish/subscribe networks", *Computer Networks*, vol. 55, no. 18, pp. 4021–4032, December 2011.

[STA 11] STAIS C., DIAMANTIS D., ARETHA C., et al., "VoPSI: voice over a publish-subscribe internetwork", *Future Network and Mobile Summit – FutureNetw*, pp. 1–8, June 2011.

[STO 03] STOICA I., MORRIS R., LIBEN-NOWELL D., et al., "Chord: a scalable peer-to-peer lookup protocol for internet applications", *IEEE/ACM Transactions on Networking*, vol. 11, no. 1, pp. 17–32, 2003.

[TAL 12] TALEBIFARD P., LEUNG V.C., "A content centric approach to dissemination of information in vehicular networks", *ACM International Symposium on Design and Analysis of Intelligent Vehicular Networks and Applications – DIVANet*, October 2012.

[TRO 10a] TROSSEN D., BICZÓK G., "Not paying the truck driver: differentiated pricing for the future internet", *Re-Architecting the Internet Workshop – ReARCH*, pp. 1-6, November 2010.

[TRO 10b] TROSSEN D., SARELA M., SOLLINS K., "Arguments for an information-centric internetworking architecture", *ACM SIGCOMM Computer Communication Review*, vol. 40, no. 2, pp. 26–33, April 2010.

[TRO 12] TROSSEN D., PARISIS G., "Designing and realizing an information-centric internet", *IEEE Communications Magazine*, vol. 50, no. 7, pp. 60–67, 2012.

[TSI 11] TSILOPOULOS C., XYLOMENOS G., "Supporting diverse traffic types in information centric networks", *ACM SIGCOMM Workshop on Information-Centric Networking – ICN*, pp. 13–18, August 2011.

[TYS 12] TYSON G., SASTRY N., RIMAC I., et al., "A survey of mobility in information-centric networks: challenges and research directions", *ACM MobiHoc Workshop on Emerging Name-Oriented Mobile Networking Design – Architecture, Algorithms, and Applications – NoM'12*, June 2012.

[UAR 12] U-AROON P., TANTATSANAWONG P., "Improving network performance of healthcare services using content-centric network model", *International Conference on Computing Technology and Information Management – ICCM*, April 2012.

[ULH 12] UL HAQUE M., PAWLIKOWSKI K., WILLIG A., et al., "Performance analysis of blind routing algorithms over content centric networking architecture", *International Conference on Computer and Communication Engineering – ICCCE*, pp. 922–927, July 2012.

[URM 09] URMSON C., BAKER C., DOLAN J., et al., "Autonomous driving in traffic: boss and the urban challenge", *AI Magazine*, vol. 30, no. 2, pp. 17–29, summer 2009.

[VAH 00] VAHDAT A., BECKER D., Epidemic routing for partially-connected ad hoc networks, Report, Duke University, July 2000.

[VAR 11] VARVELLO M., RIMAC I., LEE U., et al., "On the design of content-centric MANETs", *International Conference on Wireless On-demand Network Systems and Services – WONS*, January 2011.

[VAR 12] VARVELLO M., PERINO D., ESTEBAN J., "Caesar: a content router for high speed forwarding", *ACM SIGCOMM Workshop on Information-Centric Networking – ICN*, pp. 73–78, August 2012.

[VIS 09] VISALA K., LAGUTIN D., TARKOMA S., "LANES: an inter-domain data-oriented routing architecture", *Re-Architecting the Internet Workshop – ReARCH*, pp. 55–60, December 2009.

[WÄH 12] WÄHLISCH M., SCHMIDT T.C., VAHLENKAMP M., "Bulk of interest: performance measurement of content-centric routing", *ACM Special Interest Group on Data Communication Conference – SIGCOMM*, pp. 99–100, August 2012.

[WAL 04] WALFISH M., BALAKRISHNAN H., SHENKER S., "Untangling the Web from DNS", *USENIX/ACM Symposium on Networked Systems Design and Implementation – NSDI*, pp. 17–17, March 2004.

[WAN 99] WANG J., "A survey of Web caching schemes for the Internet", *ACM SIGCOMM Computer Communication Review*, vol. 29, no. 5, pp. 36–46, October 1999.

[WAN 04] WANG L., PARK K.S., PANG R., *et al.*, "Reliability and security in the CoDeeN content distribution network", *USENIX Annual Technical Conference – ATC*, pp. 14–14, June 2004.

[WAN 05] WANG X., YIN Y.L., YU H., "Finding collisions in the full SHA-1", *CRYPTO*, vol. 3621, pp. 17–36, 2005.

[WAN 12a] WANG J., WAKIKAWA R., KUNTZ R., *et al.*, "Data naming in vehicle-to-vehicle communications", *Workshop on Emerging Design Choices in Name-Oriented Networking – NOMEN*, pp. 328–333, March 2012.

[WAN 12b] WANG S., BI J., WU J., *et al.*, "On adapting HTTP protocol to content centric networking", *International Conference on Future Internet Technologies – CFI*, pp. 1–6, September 2012.

[WOL 99] WOLMAN A., VOELKER M., SHARMA N., *et al.*, "On the scale and performance of cooperative Web proxy caching", *ACM Symposium on Operating Systems Principles – SOSP*, December 1999.

[XIE 12] XIE M., WIDJAJA I., WANG H., "Enhancing cache robustness for content-centric networking", *IEEE Conference on Computer Communications – INFOCOM*, March 2012.

[YAN 00] YANG J., WANG W., MUNTZ R., "Collaborative Web caching based on proxy affinities", *ACM International Conference on Measurement and Modeling of Computer Systems – SIGMETRICS*, June 2000.

[ZHA 10] ZHANG L., ESTRIN D., BURKE J., *et al.*, Named data networking (NDN) Project, Report no. NDN-0001, Xerox Palo Alto Research Center – PARC, 2010.

[ZHA 11] ZHANG N., LEVÄ T., HÄMMÄINEN H., "Two-sidedness of internet content delivery", *IEEE Conference on Telecommunications Internet and Media Techno-Economics – CTTE*, pp. 16–18, May 2011.

[ZHU 10] ZHU Y., CHEN M., NAKAO A., "CONIC: content-oriented network with indexed caching", *IEEE Global Internet Symposium 2010 – GI Symposium)*, March 2010.

[ZHU 11] ZHU Z., WANG S., YANG X., *et al.*, "ACT: audio conference tool over named data networking", *ACM SIGCOMM Workshop on Information-Centric Networking – ICN*, pp. 68–73, August 2011.

Index

Printed and bound by CPI Group (UK) Ltd, Croydon, CR0 4YY

27/10/2024

14580725-0005